What people are saying ...

"In her new book of letters to prayer partners, *Going with God: Letters from Our Travels*, Priscilla Flory reveals her deep and abiding love for God and his people around the world. These heartfelt missives deal with the broad spectrum of human needs and concerns and touch on all the keys of joy in Christ, from the sublime to the whimsical. Even those who have not known and prayed with Priscilla as I have for decades cannot mistake the authenticity of her faith and her personal ministry of prayer. Her spiritual fervor and tireless outreach in the name of God are deeply inspiring and consoling. Read this book; it is good for your heart and your soul."

—M. Rev. Denis M. Garrison, Th.D., OCOSB

"When I think of Priscilla, what comes to my mind first is the scripture "His banner over me is love." Priscilla's heart for Jesus is overflowing toward all those she meets, and these letters are a reflection of that great love for her Savior and others."

—Wally Armstrong, former PGA touring professional and author of *In His Grip*

"If you are among the many privileged to count Tom and Priscilla among your friends, you know that when you spend time with them, you see the light of the Lord alive in their lives. If you are even more privileged to pray with Priscilla, you become part of a special relationship of love and intimacy she shares with the Lord. For those of us who are friends or prayer partners, this book will bring back special moments. Perhaps even better, for those who haven't had the chance to personally be a part of Priscilla's prayer times, this book will draw you in, share her heart, and challenge you to a deeper intimacy with Jesus in your own life."

—Dr. Jim Solberg, DD, M.Div., MAJCS;
USA National Director Bridges for Peace; author of *Sinai Speaks*

"Jesus said, 'Follow Me.' Priscilla and Tom Flory have been faithfully doing just that for decades on a journey that has taken them around the world. This book allows you into the middle of that journey. My heart has been singing as I read Priscilla's letters. In fact, and I don't think it is a coincidence that as I was sitting down to write this 'endorsement,' the 'Hallelujah Chorus' came shouting out in the Starbucks where I was sitting. I took it as a personal endorsement from God Himself! Let your heart sing as you join Priscilla's journey with Jesus."

—Tim Philpot, author of *Judge Z Irretrievably Broken*, former Kentucky senator and former president of CBMC International

"Priscilla has been a dear, close friend in ministry and personally. She is a woman with a deep love and passion for God that is exhibited in a meaningful prayer life that spills out in love and ministry to others selflessly. That is what this book is all about. Romans 5:5 comes to mind when I think of the place of inspiration, the Holy Spirit moving on Priscilla's heart: "And hope does not disappoint, because the love of God has been poured out within our hearts through the Holy Spirit who was given to us." Priscilla simply shares out of her personal time with God, the love that He has poured upon a heart of brokenness, a heart crying out, a heart that sees Him in everything, a heart that desires that for others too. You will be moved, encouraged, enlightened, and motivated to enjoy deeper, more meaningful relationship with the Lord Most High as a result. "Go with" her on this journey. It will take you where you never knew you needed to go."

—Victoria Boeseman, National Prayer Director Bridges for Peace

GOING *with* GOD

LETTERS FROM OUR TRAVELS

PRISCILLA FLORY

ISBN: 978-1-4834-6351-3 (sc)
ISBN: 978-1-4834-6350-6 (hc)
ISBN: 978-1-4834-6352-0 (e)

Library of Congress Control Number: 2016921365

Lulu Publishing Services rev. date: 3/30/2017

When I think of the words *extravagant love*, I think first
of my beloved heavenly Father, whom I affectionately
call “Abba,” because he says that all of his children
can have that intimacy and affection with him.

I also think of my beloved husband,
Thomas David Flory.

It is with love and gratitude that I dedicate this book to them.

Priscilla
Dear Buck, Beth and Matt —
Always "go with" God and you
will never go wrong!

Love and hugs —
Cilla
August 28, 2018

"But you will receive power when the Ruach HaKodesh comes upon you; you will be my witnesses both in Yerushalayim and in all Y'hudah and Shomron, indeed to the ends of the earth."

—Yeshua, Acts 1:8 (CJB)

"You can go anywhere in the world in your prayer closet."

—Dr. Richard C. Halverson, former Chaplain
of the United States Senate

Contents

Foreword

Every so often just the right letter or note arrives in the mail, the one we read over and over because it moves us, or makes us smile, or causes us to pause and reflect.

Personally for me those "right words" have arrived for many years in the form of Priscilla Flory's "Family Extended" newsletters. Through Priscilla's stories and illustrations of how God has powerfully and faithfully worked in her life, she helps draw us nearer to the heart of Yeshua and reminds all grown-ups of our need to still sit in the lap of our Abba's love. Like Paul's letters to his brothers and sisters in Christ, Priscilla's words encourage us to relax and reclaim his joy for our journey. Her collection of whimsical yet profoundly holy reflections helps us discover the tender and kind heart of our heavenly Father. They remind us of the truth of Proverbs 25: "Like apples of gold in settings of silver, is a word spoken in the right circumstances ... Like the cold of snow in a time of harvest is a faithful messenger to those who send him."

I'm deeply thankful to Priscilla for answering the call of her many readers to publish a collection of her letters she's mailed over the years. She is indeed a "faithful messenger" from our Father's heart!

—Carol Tyson

ACKNOWLEDGMENTS

Abba, Father, thank *you*! You are perfect in every way and I love you!

This book, our book, is the result of the fruitful labors of many people. I am grateful for each one, named and unnamed.

Thank you, Tom, my beloved husband, for your faith in me and in the book. I could not have done it without you, my precious "hound of heaven."

Thank you to all of my priceless family and friends whose stories make this book. You have increased my faith in God and in humanity. I love YOU! More importantly God loves you!

Three cheers for Emily Ellingwood, Jeanie Connell, Carol Tyson, and Celene Pumphrey for their advice, expertise and acts of service. Margaret Rundle and Glen Bradnum, thank you for encouraging me to publish my biography in a collection of my prayer letters.

Roberta Zapf, you have a great flare with a camera, and it was fun having you do my picture.

Dear Wally Armstrong, Victoria Boeseman, Denis Garrison, Tim Philpot, Jim Solberg, your words of encouragement humbled and encouraged me.

My beloved praying partners, you are the best! I hope your times with Abba blessed you immensely, and that you know more and more the height, the depth, the breadth, and the length of God's great love for you.

And, thank you, dear reader, for choosing this book from among the many that you could have chosen. May you be encouraged by the love that God has for you, and may you in turn love him with all of your heart, soul, mind, and strength.

Last, but certainly not least, three cheers for the great Lulu staff. You encouraged me every step of the way. Not only are you highly professionally skilled, but you are fun and friendly! I loved working with you! Let's do it again.

INTRODUCTION

March 11, 2013

Hello, dear reader,

Everyone worships. We are created to worship. The question becomes: who or what will I worship? Will I worship an activity, giving it "my all," pouring myself wholeheartedly into the pursuit of it? Will I give it my time, my energy, my finances? Will it become my reason to live? Will I worship power? Or fame? Fortune? Will I worship a person or group of people? Even my family or nation?

As for me, I have chosen to worship God—the God of Isra'el; the God of Avraham, Yitz'chak, and Ya'akov; the God who revealed himself in the Tanakh, the first thirty-nine books of the Holy Scriptures and the writings of the apostles.

The book you hold in your hand is a memoir of my "going with" God. I chose to "go with" him, choosing his opinions and his ways over anyone else's. I chose to "go with" him wherever he would take me. We have traveled the world together: from Baltimore, my birthplace, to Beit-Lechem/Bethlehem, his birthplace, and to Yerushalayim/ Jerusalem, the southernmost tip of Africa, Argentina, the southern tip of South America, Alaska and Sweden in the north, the Hawaiian Islands in the west, and Belarus in the east—literally to the far reaches of the earth.

My "going with" him seriously began in 1977 with prayer, and from that day, prayer—simple communication with him—became an important part of my life.

And so, dear one, I invite you to "go with" me on the glorious adventure of "going with" God. It is my hope and prayer that as you read these pages you will be inspired to "go with" God every moment of every day of your life. If you do, you will never regret it. After all, it is what we are created to do. It is worship.

How to read this book:

Although the letters are written in chronological order, they do not need to be read that way. Each letter stands on its own. You may want to start with the last one and read them in random order. Or you may choose to start at the beginning and read through. The choice is yours; "go with" your heart. "Go with" the Holy Spirit's promptings.

Each letter was written to a praying partner, someone personally known to me, who prays for me and my family and for whatever is on the heart of God. The first letters, written to "Praying Partner," marked one phase of our lives and the early phases of our praying journey.

In this phase I sent a letter and a calendar as a guide to each praying partner. We focused on praying for widows and orphans and the groups serving them. Each month we prayed for a particular continent, so each year we literally prayed around the globe.

"Magnificent One" marks a later phase, which I called "Magnificent Sevens." Magnificent Sevens came from the desire to gather folks together to fast and pray on the seventh day of the month from seven a.m. to seven p.m.

Although my desire was to have them gather at our farm's chapel, people could pray and fast wherever they were in the world. Again, they could "go with" the Spirit and their hearts.

However you choose to read these letters is clearly your choice.

You will notice that some letters have a PS, a postscript. These are thoughts, reflections, or observations that I have had recently regarding that particular letter.

Out of deep love and great respect for my Jewish Savior, Yeshua/Jesus, and my own family's Jewish roots, I have chosen to use the Jewish names of Jesus (Yeshua), Isaac (Yitz'chak), and Jacob (Ya'akov). I chose to use the Complete Jewish Bible (CJB) because it gave me a greater understanding of the biblical Jewish roots of my faith.

Pronouns for God are not capitalized, because that is how the biblical quotes are written. For the sake of continuity and ease of reading, I decided to keep that trend throughout the book. And I learned that in ancient Hebrew there were no uppercase letters, only lowercase. In no case is any disrespect to God meant.

Out of all the books you could have chosen to read, thank you for "going with" this book. May you be blessed beyond your wildest imaginings.

May you know the height, the depth, the breadth, and the length of God's great love for you.

Sincerely,

Priscilla

The Letters

1

The Constant in an Ever-Changing World

September 27, 1989

Dear Praying Partner,

Change is a word that frequently comes to mind these days. As I look around at my surroundings, as I observe the weather, and as I see the lives of so many people, one thing stands out: change. We all experience it. I am enjoying the changes I am experiencing. My mom has moved in with us, adding a new dimension to the family. Fall has arrived; it's my favorite time of the year. The crisp, cooler days are so invigorating. And I've aged another year!

Others are also experiencing change. However, for them the changes are not pleasant. In fact, they are very difficult. Families are being torn apart. Children are being abandoned. Women are deciding whether to allow the child in their womb to live or die. Hosts of people are affected by these changes.

Fortunately, there is one constant in the world: Yeshua of Nazareth. He remains the lover of souls, the healer of hurts, and the giver of all good gifts. He remains the source of life and joy and peace. He is the one who constantly intercedes for us. He never changes. He is always the same. He is the hope for the world.

May we continue to be changed into his likeness. May we continue to grow in wisdom and knowledge and love of him. May we continue to share his love with a world that so desperately needs it. I am thankful for the partnership we have in these great opportunities.

Love,

Priscilla

PS: Reflecting on these last twenty-seven years, I have seen so much change—some good and some not so good. But both are a matter of opinion. How can I really know?

One change that I know has been for the better is the fact that I love God more. I am not the same person I was twenty-seven years ago. I used to think I knew everything. I realize now how little I do know. Now I *know* that the more I know God, the more there is to know.

In this world of change, he remains the one constant. He remains the everlasting source of life, hope, joy, and peace. He is our anchor in every storm. He is worthy of all devotion.

2

The Faithful

Christmas 1996

Dear Praying Partner,

"Why did God put the Tree of the Knowledge of Good and Evil in the Garden of Eden?" This question was posed to me by a dear friend on a recent trip to Minsk, Belarus. Let's contemplate it together.

God is a loving Father who protects his children. He wanted his children to know that good and evil existed in the world, but he did not want them to experience, to *know*, evil. God is a loving Father who sets boundaries for his children and gives them the opportunity to choose to obey those boundaries. God is a loving Father who provides security for his children by proving his trustworthiness. He keeps his word, even when the cost to him is great.

When God told Adam and Eve not to eat the fruit of the Tree of the Knowledge of Good and Evil—for if they did, they would die—he took a big risk. His creation, man, might choose not to believe him, and thus choose not to obey him. He knew that this act of not trusting would sever their relationship, for without trust there could be no relationship.

God also knew what it would require to restore the broken relationship. He knew it would take a sacrifice. He knew it would take the cross. He knew it would take his giving up his life. It would not be easy. It would mean agony and suffering.

Yet he did it. Such love. Such amazing, undeserved love. This is our God. This is our Savior. This is our gift. May we embrace him wholeheartedly with childlike faith, with gratitude and with love.

You are precious and dearly loved!

With his blessings,

Priscilla

PS: Obedience, grounded in trust in him, pleases God.

3

Why Pray?

August 26, 1997

Dear Praying Partner,

The telephone rings. What a thrill when the voice on the other end says, "Hi, Mom." What a thrill when my child wants to talk with me. Wow! It doesn't matter what the reason is for the call. Just to hear that child's voice is great.

Sometimes the call is just to chat. Sometimes someone needs advice. Sometimes we have to make plans to get together. Sometimes we think the call is for one reason, and it turns out to be something entirely different from what we planned. Sometimes we need to make amends. No matter what the reason for the call is, we've been together, and that's the glory of it!

I was recently thinking about the Lord's Prayer and wondered why God would want us to pray when he already knows what we need. Why wouldn't he just give it? The thought that occurred to me was this: *He likes to hear your voice.* Amazing! The God of the universe, the one who created it all and sees it all, likes to hear my voice. And *yours.*

In discussing the question with others, some great reasons came up: Father wants us to know that he listens. God wants us to know what we are thinking, and sometimes we don't know what we think, want, or need until we start to talk with someone about it. He wants us to be able to see his involvement in our lives. Finally, he wants to evoke a response from us.

So, dear one, if you've lost heart in prayer because you think Father doesn't hear or doesn't care, don't you believe it! Just give him a call. His number is listed in the Book under Jeremiah 33:3. He says to call him, and he will tell you all kinds of wonderful things!

Thank you for your partnership in prayer. We need it, and we count on it.

You are precious and dearly loved!

Hugs,

Priscilla

PS: Have you called him lately?

I am eternally grateful for our faithful praying partners who call on God on our behalf. Priceless is their gift.

4

In Praise of Mother

December 19, 1998

Dear Praying Partner,

Harriett Buckingham Ripperger
Born: September 9, 1919
Died: December 7, 1998

Small in stature, she was a giant of a lady. Her life was marked by tragedy but lived with great joy. Although an invalid in the latter years of her life, her life was never invalid. Quite the contrary, for it was because of her later years that God became even more real to me. I had the pleasure and privilege of knowing her all my life. You see, this giant was my mother.

Sacrifice is a word that comes to mind when I think of Mother. It wasn't until I became a wife and mother that I began to understand what that word meant, and I began to appreciate that quality in her. Mother sacrificed herself for the good of others, which is quite contrary to our day when people are often more willing to sacrifice others because of selfishness.

One of her most irritating habits was one of the most important gifts she ever gave me. She had a way of always getting me to look at situations from the other person's perspective when they had hurt me. Shifting my view from me to someone else was never easy, or immediate, but it always bore the healing fruit of peace.

Mother's entry into a nursing home was one of the most difficult times of my life, because I had vowed that would never happen to her. But God was gracious in providing a wonderful home and friends for her, along with the round-the-clock care she needed.

One of Mother's most endearing qualities was her gratitude. "Thank you" was a phrase that was often heard from her lips. No gift, no service given, was too small not to receive a thank-you from her.

As we celebrate this special time of year, and remember the sanctity of human life, it is a privilege to honor and remember this lady who gave me the gift of life. Although she has passed from our view, I see her clearly in my mind's eye. She is dancing in her heavenly garments of white. She is laughing, her head held high, and she is truly enjoying the abundant life of a child of *God,* for that is who she truly is.

Loving life,

Priscilla

PS: "Honor your father and mother, so that you may live long in the land which *ADONAI* your God is giving you" (Exodus 20:12).

5

How Will I Recognize Him?

April 28, 1999

Dear Praying Partner,

A number of years ago, my daughter Ashley and I were dispatched by my daughter Emily to go to Dulles International Airport to pick up her friend who was coming from Germany to visit.

"How will we recognize her?" we asked.

Emily responded with the following description: "She's a little taller than you are, Mom. She has brown hair, and she's pretty."

She was due in at a certain time, on a certain flight. Don't you just love it? I did! Do you know how many people could have fit that description? First of all, most of the world is taller, even a little taller, than I am!

Armed with that rather sketchy bit of information, Ashley and I set off to retrieve the dear young lady. Glory to God, we did find her. And amazingly, as we waited and looked, she turned out to be the only person who could fit Emily's description.

I have been reading and studying the prophecies concerning God's promised Messiah. Centuries before he appeared, God clearly described him so that when he did come, people would be able to recognize him. I have been amazed by God's attention to detail. It's just another marvelous characteristic of our wonderful heavenly Father.

For example, God told us the sex: male. He told us the nationality: Hebrew. He told us where he would be born: Bethlehem in Judea. He gave us his family tree, very detailed. When would the Messiah be born? That was told too. Why would He come? Yes, that was described in advance also. And He included that very important detail, His name: Yeshua.

God even told us the way the Messiah would die, and he included the *most glorious news* that the Messiah would be *resurrected*. And all of the sins of the world would be paid for by his life, death, and resurrection. You and I can be free! No more guessing about whether we have done enough "good deeds" to get into heaven. No more guessing, "Is this the One?" Yeshua was everything that God the Father said his Messiah would be!

Is that good news? Don't you just love it? Mathematically speaking, the chances of one person fulfilling just a few of those prophetic details are astronomical, and Yeshua fulfilled them all. For me, the prophecies and their fulfillment are the most conclusive evidence that Yeshua is who he said he was.

The Bible is to me a most remarkable book. God chose so many people to write down his message, and not all at once either. The message, however, is consistent throughout. God consistently shows that he is involved. He is alive. He speaks. He listens. He acts. He is committed. He is trustworthy. He is awesome! He is worthy to be thanked and praised.

It is for this reason that we seek him and his plans for us, and the wisdom to carry them out. We seek his will for the women and children we desire to serve. Father really does know best!

We come to a wonderful and mighty God. Come and stay a spell with him, dear one. Let him tell you great and mighty things that he alone can tell you. All will be blessed.

You are most precious and so dearly loved. Abba said so.

6

Seeing Abba in Germany and Belarus

June 24, 1999

Dear Praying Partner,

When I was a little girl, one of my passions was reading. I remember riding my bike to the old bookmobile that used to come near our house so I could load up on books. Two of my all-time favorites were *Heidi* and *The Secret Garden*. I loved the fact that healing took place in the gardens of love that were the heart of each of these books. Even as an adult I am constantly reminded of them and their message. Words, ideas, and messages are great gifts which God has given to us as the heart and soul of books.

Our recent trip to Belarus and Germany was like a wonderful book authored by our wonderful God and Father. When I think of our trip, words come to mind, such as *humility, faithfulness, awesome, provider, celebrate, enduring, love, friendship, hospitality, surprises*, and *serendipity.*

In Germany Tom and I met up with two of our praying partners. Tom and I had been enjoying our annual golf retreat with friends from Germany and the USA. We have been doing that for a number of years, and it is thrilling to see the deepening relationships we have there. Meeting new folks is fun too. The hospitality we experienced in Germany, both at the beginning and at the end of our trip, was so gracious, warm, and *fun*.

The celebration of Hope Home's birthday in Minsk, Belarus, was a wonderful event: a celebration of the faithfulness of our great God and the wonderful people he has chosen to nurture the precious children there.

I was told that I would be asked to speak during the program, but I couldn't imagine why, so I dismissed the idea. The party was in full swing. People were obviously enjoying themselves. There were a number of speeches, and lots of conversation. Suddenly, I heard my name being mentioned from the podium. The emcee wanted me to come and share remarks. I was stunned! What could I possibly have to say to these precious people? I looked at them. What was I to say?

"I came to Belarus to see Jesus," I began. A hush fell over the room at the mention of his name. I told them that I had seen him in the love I saw at the orphanage. I had seen him in the love I experienced through people there. I thanked them, prayed, and sat down. I could hardly believe what had just happened.

When I was a little girl, I was told that people in the Soviet Union were our enemies. But here in this little secret garden, love abounded. We were family, united by our love for children. It was a most precious moment.

Yes, we saw Vi, one of the precious children at Hope Home, and we all had special chances to be with him. He's growing by leaps and bounds, a wonderful little boy.

The latest news on his adoption/medical process is that the government won't allow him to leave except for a permanent adoption! I see this as a very positive step, because it makes the choices of what needs to be done very clear, specific, and ordered. How much more wonderful it would be for Vi to be settled in a family while undergoing the medical routines that will be necessary to fix his little body. How wonderful for him to have the security of a family and not be moved from place to place.

So, where is the family of God's choice for Vi? That is the all-important question! Please do not lose heart in praying.

I wish I could tell you of all the wonders God did, and what we saw that He is doing, but ... it would take a book.

I hope that you have a great summer. I'd love to hear from you, if you have a moment or two. Please know that you are precious and dearly, dearly loved.

Hugs from the garden,

Priscilla

PS: What happened to Vi? See "The Ultimate Family Man", Letter # 22.

7

It's Thanksgiving!

November 24, 1999

Dear Praying Partner,

It's the day before Thanksgiving, and I am keenly aware that there are many things to be grateful for. You are a gift, and I thank God for you. Your partnership in prayer on behalf of our friends and family members is a wonderful gift. Thank you.

Thanks be to God that Yeshua came to earth to show us what God, the Father and Creator of all, is like. Thanks be to God that his desire is to have a relationship with us, and that he came to tell us in words and actions.

Thanks be to God for the bonds that hold us to him and to each other. I love his bonds, for they provide security, which gives way to confidence and great freedom.

Thanks be to God for the bonds of *love,* which never constrict, never stifle, but instead provide truth, allow diversity, and never fail.

Thanks be to God for the bonds of prayer, which unite our hearts in harmonious conversation with one another and with the Creator, the LORD, God Almighty.

Thanks be to God for the bonds of purpose: to bring before his throne of grace the praises and petitions of family and friends who live throughout the world.

Thanks be to God for the bonds of family and friends, and for the power and strength these bonds afford us.

Thanks be to God for the material gifts he has given to us and for the opportunities we have to share our goods with those who are in need.

Finally, thanks be to God that he exists in this world. It is, after all, his world, created for his pleasure and purposes.

As this century draws to a close and a new one begins, I am excited to see what God will do with us. One thing that I have learned over the last half of this century is that Father really does know best; and because he is love and has bound us to himself, we can rest assured that, whatever happens, he will be with us, and it will ultimately be for our good.

God loves you. He said so, and I believe him.

Love and hugs are flying your way,

Priscilla

8

The Last Words of the Twentieth Century

December 28, 1999

Dear Praying Partner,

"Well, Mrs. Flory, what kind of a job do you want?" asked the employment agency manager. I really didn't want a job, but I heard myself say, "I'd like to have one with my own office where I can have flowers and pictures of my family all around."

"Oh, you'd like an executive position," he replied. "Yes," I said. Then he said, "Well, we'll see what we can do."

That conversation took place almost thirty-five years ago, shortly after Tom and I were married. He was in the US Navy and gone, gone, gone. How would I spend my time with him always away? A job seemed like the perfect answer, but Tom didn't want me to have a job, and quite frankly, neither did I. One thing was clear: I could not sit around and watch TV and eat bonbons all day!

The man from the employment agency never found me that executive position, and I forgot the entire conversation until a few years ago—and until now. God never forgot it. He began to fill my life with his plans and his people.

As I write this letter to you today, I am sitting in my office, surrounded by beautiful flowers and pictures of my family. I still don't have a job! What I do have is far greater to me: I have a wonderful worldwide family. I can see their faces, I can tell you their names. I can see where they live, places that are real to me because I've been to visit. We have prayed for each other and played together. Some are older—some much older—and some are much younger than I. We speak different languages. We are different colors. We celebrate holidays in different styles. There is one constant: God is our Father. It is he who created us. He brought us together and keeps us together. It is his plan for us that we desire.

I am so grateful that God took my words and gave them flesh. I am so glad that he took the intangible and made it tangible. I am grateful that he took his intangible Word and made him tangible so that we could see him, touch him, hear him, and experience him.

As we enter the new millennium, I wonder what God has in store for us, individually and as his family. Some things we know; others are uncertain. One thing is sure: he knows best.

Let us proceed with confidence and joy, knowing that God loves us and desires a loving relationship with us. Let us go forth with the assurance that we are very precious and very dearly loved, for that is what he said, and I believe him.

Hugs for the new millennium,

Priscilla

PS: We are now well into the second decade of the new millennium. In each decade Abba has expanded my relationships, most recently in Israel and California, from one side of the globe to the other.

With each new relationship and each experience comes a deeper appreciation for God, his ways, and his activity in this world, which so desperately needs him.

9

Building Bridges

January 24, 2000

Hello, dear Praying Partner,

It is so much fun to be part of a big family that has so many loving, caring, dedicated people. This month, and in the next few months, you will be hearing from some of them.

When Tom, our children, and I began inviting women and children in crisis to come and live with us, we had no idea what God would do with all of us! Isn't it wonderful how God tells us just what we need to know when we need to know it? He is so wise!

Twenty years ago an invisible wall existed between our nation and the Soviet Union. I never thought it would be possible to visit any of its republics.

Today I count it a privilege to have traveled to Belarus, a former republic, six times. Some of my dearest friends live there, and together we are building bridges between the people of our nations. In the process, we are experiencing God.

Thank you for being a bridge-builder through prayer. It is my hope that you will continue to pray for us. Most of all, I hope that you will experience all the blessings that our wonderful Father has in store for you. You really are precious, you know!

Love and hugs for the New Year,

Priscilla

10

Mourning into Joy

January 26, 2000

Thanks be to Thee, O Lord, God,
for You have turned my sorrow into joy and my
mourning into dancing;
for she who was lost is found. And she who was dead is
now alive!
—Priscilla Flory

Hello, dear Praying Partner,

I am writing this letter to you because you are an important part of my world, and because I want you to know the wonderful things that God has done for Tom and me. I hope that you will share our joy.

Thirty-four years ago, before the birth of our son David, we had a miscarriage. The doctor assured me that I didn't need to cry, for I would certainly be able to have children. I was young, only twenty-three. After all, his own wife had had a number of miscarriages before she was able to carry a baby to full term!

My tears unnerved Tom. What was I to do with the sadness and feelings of guilt I was experiencing? I thought that surely I had done something to have had this happen. What should I do? Stuff those thoughts and feelings, "gather myself together," "be a big girl," and "get on with life"? Would time heal my hurt as people said it would?

Thirty-four years after the loss of our baby, God, in his infinite mercy and grace, has brought me healing, taking away the pain of loss and releasing me from guilt. He has introduced me to our daughter, whose very, very brief life has profoundly affected me.

Last Saturday, the twenty-second of January, Tom and I participated in a seminar on post abortion healing. Tom was most impressed that with the legalization of abortion the life of the unborn child has been devalued, and that the devaluation transfers to those babies who are miscarried as well.

The seminar was followed by a beautiful memorial service to honor the babies who had died because of abortion, miscarriage, or stillbirth.

I had been excited to go, and when Emily had asked me to lead the group in some singing, I'd been thrilled. We talked about what we thought might happen, and I mentioned my miscarriage. "Maybe God will tell you the sex and the name of the baby, Mom," she said. I laughed. I certainly hoped so.

God is faithful. Last Thursday, January 20, God did reveal to us the sex of the baby and the name we should give her. We asked. He gave. No, it wasn't an audible voice; it was a thought that came with great conviction, peace, and joy. Our baby was a girl, and her name was to be Harriett Elizabeth. *Harriett* was after my mother, and *Elizabeth* means "set apart for God." That was an important thing for me to realize, because it took away the sting of losing her. After all, she was God's gift to us; it was he who had created her and set her apart for himself. Her life had purpose and meaning, and she would be with him.

This is all very fresh and new, so I am amazed by what I'm learning every day. Harriett has come alive to me. Just to be able to think about her is new and precious. To be able to talk about her is wonderful. The knowledge that she is at peace, experiencing God's presence, is too marvelous for words. The recognition of her place in our family is so important.

I am grateful. I am grateful for this babe, whose existence and death have helped me to understand those who have suffered losses like ours, especially those who have experienced the tragedy of abortion. To whom can they talk about their sadness and guilt? Who will hold them when they cry?

I am grateful for David, Emily, and Ashley, our precious children, who have become the most wonderful adults and bring us such great joy.

I am grateful for my beloved husband, who has learned to allow me to cry, and to just hold me while the tears flow.

I am grateful to our wonderful creator, to whom all of life is precious and to whom the death of anyone is so important. I am grateful that he can turn sorrow into joy, mourning into dancing, and death into life.

Thank you for allowing me to share these thoughts and events with you; it has made them all the sweeter.

Loving you,

Priscilla

PS: The idea for "Good Mourning" came from this conference. In Good Mourning conferences we teach people that godly grief is a good thing, and that there is a comforter and counselor who will walk with them through the process and turn their sorrow into joy. We have been privileged to teach Good Mourning in the USA, South Africa, Belarus, Israel, and Hungary.

As men and women learn to discuss their loss and grief, they find freedom and healing.

11

The Heart of the Savior

March 12, 2000

Dear Praying Partner,

It happened on a Thursday evening in January, 1998. Our couples' group gathered at our home. As was our usual custom, we talked about things that we wanted others to pray about. It was my turn, and I surprised myself by saying, "Please pray that God will remove anti-Semitism from the church." I had recently heard a racial slur about Jewish people that pained me.

Was that all there was to anti-Semitism: racial slurs? Or was there more to it than that? What exactly was I praying for? Was I anti-Semitic in any way? That prayer catapulted me onto a most amazing journey of discovery, which took me back to the biblical roots of my faith.

One thing I learned about being "anti" anything is that it is not just hatred of or being against someone or something. It can involve abandonment, replacement, or rejection. Our lips reveal our hearts.

Tom and I have just read the seventeenth chapter of the book of John. I remembered that Yeshua's first students and followers were Jewish. Yeshua Himself was Jewish. I love His Hebrew name, *Yeshua*. And his surname is not "Christ."

I think of the events that we will celebrate in April: Yeshua's death and resurrection, events that took place at the Jewish feasts of Passover and the Feast of First Fruits.

Is it just coincidence that Yeshua, our Passover Lamb was sacrificed at the same time that the Jews were celebrating Passover? Is it just coincidence that Yeshua rose on the Feast of First Fruits, and that he is declared to be the first fruits of the brethren? I don't think so. One thing is sure: God's timing is always perfect; nothing is coincidental or accidental!

Yeshua's prayer in John, chapter seventeen, is perhaps my favorite chapter in all of scripture. It is such a beautiful picture of the heart of our Savior, the Messiah. Perhaps the most important and most striking element is his desire that we all be one, just as he and the Father are one. His desire is for our unity—with him and with others.

It has been said that the greatest schism in mankind is that between Jews and Gentiles. I believe Yeshua was praying for the healing of that division. I believe that his desire is that we all, Jews and Gentiles, will recognize that he is the long-awaited Messiah, and that our common faith and unity in him will unite us as well. Our unity in him would show the world that he exists, and that he is who he says he is!

Prayer: There is great power in prayer. It puts us in touch with the one who is all-powerful. It puts us in touch with the one who shares that power with his children. It puts us in touch with the one whose power is *love.*

Love is the heart of Yeshua's prayer. His prayer was born out of love. It was said in love. Its desire is for love. May we be the answer to his prayer as we love others and ourselves, trust him, and are reconcilers.

"Oh, Lord, may thy will be done on earth as it is in heaven, and let it begin with me." Amen?

Because He loved us first,

12

A Salute to Mothers

April 26, 2000

Dear Praying Partner,

Mom, Mumsy, Momma, Pris, Priscilla, Mother, and Gigi: These words are music to my ears, because they are the names that reflect who I am to my children and grandchildren. I am happy and grateful to have been able to give birth to David, Emily, and Ashley. Martha, Tom, and Greg are their delightful spouses. They too are my children, by marriage.

God has gifted Tom and Emily with children, and I am now, happily, a grandmother: "Gigi" to Alexandra and Megan. I am called "Mother" by a young man living in Rwanda at the Imbabazi Orphanage. I feel like he has adopted me. Isn't that a wonderful turnabout? What joy! Birth, marriage, and adoption have brought me the joy of motherhood.

God tells us that we are to honor our father and mother, and that if we do, we will be blessed. Isn't it interesting that he doesn't say to do this just once a year, or if we feel like it, or if our parents deserve it? After all, where would any of us be without our mothers?

Once again, God shows us his infinite wisdom. In unconditionally valuing someone else, we get blessed! Honor gives birth to gratitude. Gratitude births joy. Joy gives birth to life. That is blessing.

The commandment to honor our father and mother promises blessing. The blessing is long life—not just existence, not just survival, but life!

In her biography, *Land of a Thousand Hills*, Rosamond Carr talked about her desire to have children. Although Roz had always wanted children, she and her husband Kenneth had never had any of their own. Then, at age eighty-two, when she was least expecting it, God gave her forty all at once: orphans of the tragic Rwandese genocide.

Roz is an extraordinary woman with a heart as big as Africa, where she and about one hundred children make their home, "Imbabazi." Emily and I were immediately drawn to her when we met her in Rwanda in 1995. Her love for the children was obvious. Her concern for their welfare was evident. What was most appealing to me, though, was the fact that Roz used her own home to care for the children. She used what she had—her home, her time, her talents, and her business—to support the children.

Imbabazi means, "A place where you can find the love that a mother would give." At Imbabazi many children find the love of a mother. Rosamond Carr loves each one as though they are her very own, and by God's grace, they are.

One day when we were talking, Roz mentioned that the children of Imbabazi needed wool for their knitting projects. Prayer partner Sheila immediately came to mind. Sheila is a knitter par excellence! Many babes have been warmed by the beautiful blankets created by Sheila's flying fingers.

It wasn't long after I mentioned the need for wool that Sheila telephoned to say that she had some to give the children. I expected a few skeins. Not so! Sheila had amassed quite a number of beautifully colored and textured skeins of wool. Such a great gift. I could hardly wait to send it to Roz and the children.

Mailing the wool was an adventure. The helpful young man at the parcel post store dutifully filled my request for shipping and informed me that the shipping cost would be over four hundred dollars. "Surely there must be some mistake," I gasped. No, he informed me, it was the size of the box. My heart sank. How would the wool get to Roz and the children? Something had to be done, but what?

The resourceful young man asked what I was shipping. Could it be squeezed into a smaller box? Fortunately, wool can be squeezed without hurting it. After much cutting and retaping of the box, the wool was ready to go!

The other day we received a wonderful letter from Roz. The wool arrived just in time for the children's spring vacation, and they needed something to do. With the arrival of the wool, the children could knit and make items to sell. Once again, God reminded us of his wonderful provision and his impeccable timing. And don't you just love his sense of humor?

I recently had the privilege of attending the memorial service of a very dear friend. As family and friends gathered to honor and remember the life of this dear lady, we gave thanks to God for her.

Our love for God, prayer, and my family were just some of the many things she and I had in common. We had also shared the sorrow of miscarriage.

A number of people remarked that my friend was childless, in the sense that she had never given birth to her own children. My heart screamed within me, "She *did* have children. She *did* have children. Just because they didn't live long enough to give credence to their reality didn't mean that they had never existed!"

Perhaps these dear people didn't know about the miscarriages. That would not be strange, because my friend was a very private person. Besides, miscarriages are often downplayed by doctors, patients, family, and friends alike.

So many people have experienced the grief of pregnancy loss, abortion, miscarriage, and stillbirth. Many are still captured by it. Praise God that through Good Mourning we have the opportunity to bring healing and release to the captives.

Praise God! We have the opportunity to help turn mourning into joy.

So, dear one,

Cheers to mothers!
Hip, hip, hooray!
Cheers to life!
Hip, hip, hooray! Hip, hip, hooray!

Love and hugs are flying your way,

Priscilla

13

The Great Heart of a Child

May 27, 2000

Dear Praying Partner,

March 1990, Lima, Peru

She was beautiful as she strode purposefully through the hotel lobby. She immediately caught my eye, and I thought how much I would like to know her. Impossible, I thought. She's a stranger I'll never know.

March 2000, Buenos Aires, Argentina

She is still beautiful. She is no longer a stranger but a dear friend. Tom and I went to Buenos Aires to visit her, her family and friends, and her beautiful nation, Argentina. Who is she? She is my friend Ewa.

We met in 1990 in Lima, Peru, through a mutual friend. We were all in Peru because of our desire to serve orphans there. The trip was a life-changing one for me because of the many ways I experienced God at every turn. Ewa was one of the blessings of the trip. She would introduce me to her part of the world.

Shortly after our arrival in Buenos Aires, I met Juliana. Juliana is no bigger than a minute, but she has a heart as big as all outdoors. She is the perfect example of the widow's mite, except for the fact that she isn't a widow! She is two and a half years old. She lives in a slum, and her view is of a garbage dump.

The nearby river and the breezes bring the foul odors of the animal slaughterhouse that is just up river from where she lives.

Her home is not filled with material luxuries, as you might imagine. So, imagine my amazement as Juliana handed me her stuffed tiger, her only toy, her gift to me. Amazing, simply amazing. This little girl, whom many would consider poor, is so rich in spirit. Her generosity still overwhelms me, and I can only thank God for her.

Tom and I went to Argentina to see Ewa and her precious family. We saw God. We saw him in each one of them. We saw him in the hospitality extended by so many. We saw him in the projects that his children are doing. We heard him through words of love and encouragement. Yes, we experienced God. Praise him.

May you experience him as he extends his loving, fatherly arms to you, because you are precious and so dearly loved.

Hugs,

Priscilla

PS: I have not seen Juliana since that day, yet I remember her act of love every time I see that stuffed tiger. One little girl. One act of great sacrificial love. Bless her, Father.

14

The Value of One

June 20, 2000

Dear Praying Partner,

The invitations for the "Mourning to Joy" workshop went out, and the doubts rolled in. What if no one came? What if I had not heard God? What if? What if?

The first response came in, and I was ecstatic. Then there was nothing (for what seemed like an eternity) except the questions. What if only this lady planned to come? Would it be worth doing for only one?

June 3 dawned: a beautiful, bright spring day. The team was assembled, ready, and so excited to see what the day would bring. We looked forward to meeting our guests who would be coming for the Mourning to Joy workshop and memorial service. Yes, twenty guests were coming! We were excited to meet with God, our unseen host.

He did not disappoint us. His presence could be felt. He spoke to us through his Word and through each other. He reached out and unlocked doors that had been closed for far too long, freeing us from fear, doubt, grief, and guilt. He comforted. He healed.

Would it have been worth doing for only one person? Yes! You see, we had intended to do it for one—the one who loves us unconditionally. And we did it for each one who came, because each one is precious to God.

You, dear one, are precious, and you are very dearly loved. Thank you for praying with us and for being such an important part of this very special day.

With love and hugs,

Priscilla

PS: The "Mourning to Joy" workshop became the "Good Mourning" conferences, which teach biblical principles of grief. Many circumstances produce grief, such as the death of a loved one, divorce (which is the death of a family), and loss of any kind. Good Mourning is designed to help us go through the process of grief and not be stuck in our loss.

15

Loving God, Loving People, Loving Life!

August 11, 2000

Dear Praying Partner,

Thank you for praying for me when I asked you to pray concerning an opportunity that was offered to me. I have decided to take it.

I was asked to be the leader of the sanctity-of-life, pro-life ministry of our church, because the present leader wanted to step down. She wanted a new and fresh vision for the church's pro-life ministry. The Family Extended, would fill that desire.

What does it mean to be pro-life? What is a pro-life ministry? To some people it simply means that they are against abortion and will do whatever they can to stop it. To others it means helping women who find themselves pregnant when they don't want to be pregnant.

The Family Extended, is a pro-life *lifestyle*. And what does that mean to us? It means that we love people! We love newly conceived people and old people. We love people who have disabilities and people who don't have disabilities. We love people who have had tragedies in their lives, such as divorce and abortion. The one thing they all have in common is that they are alive. We recognize and respect the value of every living person. And out of that love comes the desire and ability to serve them in whatever way we can.

Where does this love come from? It comes from only one source: the author of life himself, God.

Let us remember, dear one, that life—all of it—began long before there was even one man or one woman. It began with our loving, living, and eternal *God*. It flows from his life into us and through us. Life is his gift to us. That is why it is precious. That is why we can love it. That is why we can respect all persons, no matter what their age, condition, or lot in life.

I am excited about this new opportunity, because I know that in the process we will experience God. I am excited because we will grow in wisdom and knowledge and love of him. We will thank him, and we will praise him. And we will love and serve people.

You are truly precious and most dearly loved.

Hugs,

Priscilla

16

Grace and Healing

October 24, 2000

Bless *Adonai*, my soul,
and forget none of His benefits.
Psalm 103:2

Dear Praying Partner,

It is a good and joyful thing to be thankful, and we have so much to be thankful for this year. God has been so gracious to allow us to experience him as he has invited us to join him in his activities. He has taught us, provided for us, and disciplined us.

Thanks be to God for his gracious healing, which we saw this year in the lives of men and women who have experienced pregnancy loss. As for those who experienced an abortion, we rejoiced with them as they experienced God's forgiveness as he freed them of their guilt and shame. With those who experienced other losses, we rejoiced as they were able to grieve and find peace in the mourning process. In all, we saw God's amazing grace and goodness.

We are excited, very excited, about the opportunities we see to continue bringing God's grace and healing to those who grieve. We are excited about the survey, which will go out soon. It is designed to teach us about the needs of people who have experienced a pregnancy loss so we can be available to meet those needs. Thanks be to God for his wonderful gifts.

Thanks be to God that his Word can be trusted. He says that he puts those who are alone in families. Again, we thank God for bringing Sandy and Vi together to become a new family. We are grateful for all the resources God is bringing together so that Sandy can adopt Vi. May the adoption be completed in God's time.

As always, we thank God for your partnership in prayer. Your participation is crucial to all that we do.

We belong to an awesome God, who is intimately involved with his children, who remembers our frailties and gives us his strength. Let us rejoice and be glad in him.

May you enjoy all the blessings that God has in store for you today and every day. You are truly precious and most dearly loved.

Grateful for your existence,

Priscilla

PS: May God use me, and all of us, to bring his message of forgiveness, healing, and hope to those who need to hear it so that they may experience his great blessings.

17

The Gifts of Love

Christmas 2000

Dear Praying Partner,

At the first Christmas, God gave himself so that we might receive these gifts:

- Eternal life
- Friendship with him
- A Father who loves us unconditionally
- A Father-child relationship with him
- A brother, Yeshua, who loves us unconditionally and constantly prays for us
- A companion who sticks with us through thick and thin
- Hope that all things can work out for the good
- Joy in all circumstances, happy or sad, "good" or "bad"
- Plans for the future that are good
- Healing and comfort
- Peace
- Above all, *love*

All these gifts are offered to us. May we receive them with joy, humility, and gratitude.

Be blessed remembering the birth, death, and resurrection of the one who made it all possible, Yeshua himself.

You are a gift, precious and dearly loved.

Hugs,

Priscilla

18

The Treasure of Teachers

March 17, 2001

Dear Praying Partner,

Greetings from Africa!

Yesterday I received the children's March prayer calendar from Lexy and Emily and was delighted to see that it was all about teachers! You can imagine how excited I was to see that we have been thinking about the same things, even though we are more than nine thousand miles apart. You see, all month I have been thinking about the wonderful men and women who have impacted my life because of what they taught me. I would like to introduce you to a number of them.

The first one is a lady. Her name is Helen Coen, and she was my third grade teacher. She was a seed planter. She planted in me the seeds of love for the nations of the world. She had a way of making the world come alive.

She introduced me to Africa. I remember studying the Zulu people in her class; they seemed like giants to me. Many years later, I would have the pleasure of meeting a beautiful Zulu lady and her husband.

Thank you, God, for Helen.

The second teacher I'd like to recognize is also a lady and a very dear friend who introduced me to South Africa. In fact, she is the first African I ever met. Her name is Mary Main.

Tom and I just spent three days with her and her wonderful husband, Ross, in their beautiful South African home.

Mary and Ross watered the seeds that Helen planted in me. They introduced us to many of their friends, who have each added to my love and understanding of this fascinating country.

I think the most important lesson that Mary has taught me is to listen to God. Listening is that critical component of prayer that requires hearing, understanding, trust, and response.

Naecarma Goldschmitt taught me how to teach. Perhaps more importantly, she taught me how to discipline. Her lessons, taught to me when I was only nineteen, remain with me to this day, and I am now seventy-two.

She taught me to always discipline with a positive statement: "Johnny, stop that" instead of "Johnny, don't do that." Her reasoning was simple: "When we are told we can't do something, that is when we want to do it." That helped me understand something very important about God and myself. Among what are known as the Ten Commandments, God gave eight negative commands. That puzzled me, as it seemed to contradict Naecarma's teachings, and what she taught me seemed so right-on. *But* it shows our rebellious nature and our need for a savior. Ultimately I learned about God's grace and mercy.

That brings me to the most important teacher of all, Yeshua himself. Not only did he teach his students what to do, but he told them to go and teach others what he had taught them.

Today I thank God for Helen, Mary, and Naecarma. I thank God for my parents and grandparents. I thank God for the men and women who gave their lives so that I might be educated. And I thank God that our daughter Emily and her daughter Lexy listened to him and are wonderful reminders that teachers are valuable gifts from God. I would also like to applaud the teachers in our family: our daughter Ashley, her husband Greg, and my sister Harriett.

To him who alone is wise be all honor, glory, and praise. To you, dear one, his *shalom*.

Love and hugs are flying your way from Africa,

Priscilla

PS: Naecarma was my student teacher, and I had the privilege of serving on the same elementary school staff with her.

19

I Love You This Much

May 19, 2001

> The LORD descended to the top of Mount Sinai and called Moses to the top of the mountain. So Moses went up and the LORD said to him …
> —Exodus 19:20–21a

Dear Praying Partner,

Those words rang in my ears day after day during our recent trip to Africa and Israel. The trip was truly a "mountaintop" experience as Tom and I traveled in South Africa and Israel, and as Emily and Linda Nevins joined us in Rwanda and Kenya.

In Cape Town, Tom and I stayed with friends in the shadow of Table Mountain. In Rwanda we were in the "Land of a Thousand Hills," as Rwanda is known, in the shadow of the mountains there. In Israel we were in Yerushalayim, God's holy city, on Mount Zion. And in every place God spoke to us and showed himself to us in wonderful ways.

One of the clearest and most precious times occurred on the last day of our trip. Tom and I were in Yerushalayim. It was Monday. We had just celebrated Passover, and Good Friday was soon to take place. I was in the Old City with a new friend, and we were on our way home when we discovered that we had missed a turn. We found ourselves in a part of the city where we did not want to be. Time was getting short, and her feet hurt!

Thinking that a taxi would be the quickest way home, we engaged a taxi driver, who assured us that he knew where we wanted to go. We hopped into the taxi and settled back. Instead of going in the direction we wanted to go, he went exactly the opposite way! The traffic was horrific, with cars going every which way and horns blasting. So much for a relaxing ride!

All my senses perked up as anxiety attacked! Would we get home in time for prayer? Would we get home in time to get the plane? Where was he going? Why was he going in the wrong direction when he had assured us that he knew where we wanted to go? Questions, questions. Where were the answers?

Suddenly I looked at the car in front of us, a small station wagon. On the rear windshield were the words "No Fear," and underneath the words was a red heart with an arm sticking out of either side. On the heart were the words "I loved you this much." I could hardly believe what my eyes were seeing! God, our wonderful God, had just given me exactly what I needed: the assurance of his love, his presence, his intimacy, and his grace. Oh, my! He is the best, the very best!

I showed my companion, and we chuckled and relaxed once again. Immediately the taxi driver made a turn and headed in the proper direction. In no time, we were safely home.

Along the way, we had learned that our driver loved Yeshua. Why had he gone in the wrong direction? David, the driver, had been looking for an opportunity to turn around, but the traffic had made it impossible until the time that he did!

The last time Yeshua was with his disciples, he assured them that they would be his witnesses in Yerushalayim, Judea, and to the ends of the earth. It is the witness's duty and privilege to tell what he has seen and heard. And so, dear one, it is my duty and privilege to tell you that Yeshua loved you so much that he stretched out his arms on the cross, and in so doing, he said, "I love you this much."

Hugs,

Priscilla

PS: Love so amazing, so divine, who can fathom its riches? Love so amazing, so divine, demands to be shared. The world needs the love of God—not lust, not emotional warm fuzzies, but real, honest love—God's love.

20

Freedom!

June 21, 2001

So if the Son frees you, you will really be free!
—John 8:36

Dear Praying Partner,

On Wednesday, July 4, we in the USA will celebrate our Independence Day. There will be fireworks, family picnics, and the perennial sales. In thinking about the Fourth of July, I am reminded that our ancestors fought for freedom. They wanted to be free of a tyrannical king, and they wanted to be able to govern themselves. They wanted a change of ruler. They were willing to risk everything, even their lives, for the cause of freedom. They were committed, and they were willing to pay the price. Because of their sacrifices, we live in a country where we can make our own choices about how we will live. Because of their sacrifices, we can participate in the governing of our nation.

This makes me think of the scripture verse above: "So if the Son frees you, you will really be free!" Once again I am reminded of the one who wanted freedom from a tyrannical ruler: sin. He wanted it, not for himself, because he was sinless, but for you and me, because we were sinful.

Again I am reminded of the commitment. He loved us so much that he was willing to give his life for us, so that we too could have a change of ruler, a change of heart and lifestyle.

This Saturday, June 23, The Family Extended will host Good Mourning, a healing conference. It is designed to bring freedom to those who are burdened by loss. It is also designed to teach us how to serve those who are bereaved, no matter what loss might be the cause of the bereavement.

I am very excited by what I see happening through these conferences. People are having heavy burdens lifted. They are finding healing for their broken hearts. They are finding hope in Yeshua, the Savior, our consummate Comforter. And they are finding true freedom, which brings peace, joy, and hope.

I hope that as you contemplate the Fourth of July, you will also contemplate John 8:36: "So if the Son frees you, you will really be free!" And if you are heavily burdened in any way, please cast those cares upon him, as he told us to, and enjoy the peace, the joy, and the amazing love and grace that only his freedom can give you.

Hugs for freedom,

21

The Light in the Darkness

September 28, 2001

Dear Praying Partner,

On September 11, 2001, Tom and I were in Ottawa, Canada, where he was scheduled to play in the Canadian Senior Amateur Golf tournament that began that day. I was invited to a brunch for the ladies and had just arrived at the club where it was held. Except for the voices on the TV, the room was still as I entered. People were riveted to the television. I wondered what could possibly be holding their attention.

When I looked at the television, I couldn't comprehend what I was seeing, because the image was too terrible. The World Trade Center was being attacked by our own planes! Stunned, I began to cry. I couldn't move. Then my friend Shirley came over to me and gave me a big hug. Grief and comfort mingled. Other ladies offered the comfort of their arms and their condolences. Seeing my emotional state, they insisted on driving me home when I needed to leave. I was overwhelmed by their love.

The terrorist activities of September 11 changed our nation. As individuals and as a nation, we will never be the same.

On Wednesday Emily said that, in light of the events of Tuesday, she thought we needed to have another Good Mourning conference. I knew she was right, but I couldn't do anything about it! I couldn't do anything about anything. I couldn't even pray. Such can be the nature of grief.

On September 16 and 17, God gave Tom and me two very precious gifts: a granddaughter, Isabella Lucia Flory, and a grandson, Lucas Stanley Bodkins. *Lucia* means "bringer of light." *Lucas* means "bringing light." I am confident that God is raising up two new towers in Isabella and Lucas, who will bring his light to give comfort and solace to those in need.

You light up my life, dear partner, and I thank God for you. You really are precious and dearly loved, you know.

Hugs,

Priscilla

22

The Ultimate Family Man

October 18, 2001

God, in his holy dwelling,
is a father to orphans and defender of widows.
God gives homes to those who are alone
Psalm 68: 6(5)-7(6)a

Dear Praying Partner,

Praise God from whom all blessings flow. Sandy plans to board a plane on Saturday, October 27, 2001, to go to Minsk, Belarus, to complete Vi's adoption and bring him home. Hallelujah! Yes, God is good . . . all the time.

Through the power of the Holy Spirit of God, prayer, perseverance, and patience have won the day! Throughout this entire adoption process, God called us to pray and consult with him about every detail. He encouraged us to keep on keeping on, even when it seemed futile and we were tired. He gave us patience during the long periods of waiting. And now, after five years, it looks as though the end is near.

To God be the glory; great things he has done. He gave us the opportunity to work with him in the adoption process. He found just the right family for Vi, demonstrating the faithfulness of his Word, and proving that he can be trusted. He chose a son for Sandy. He built faith in us as we prayed. He assured us of the right path when we questioned. And now it looks as though Vi will soon be here among us! Praise God!

When the process began, my friend Dr. Howard Frost asked me a question: "Priscilla, why would you spend so much time, effort, and money on just one child when there are so many who need assistance?" I replied that it was what Yeshua would do. If I were the only human who needed rescuing from sin and death, he would still have come, and he would have died for only me. I still believe that is true. However, I have come to see something else.

We did not do this for only one child. No, the process has been for all of us who have prayed and participated in the process in any number of ways. You see, dear one, God wants us all to experience him, to know him in all his ways, which are so wonder-filled. And out of our experiencing him, we are to tell the world of our wonderful God and Savior. We truly have a story to tell to the nations, a story of God's wonderful love and faithfulness. Blessed be he. God cares about the entire world, and so should we.

Thank you for your prayers, which have touched God's heart. He has blessed us all.

Hugs from the heart,

Priscilla

PS: Vi was officially adopted by Sandy on October 30, 2001. Yahoo! And when he was asked where he wanted to eat to celebrate his adoption, it was at McDonald's in Minsk, Belarus. That was what he wanted, and that was what he got. Yahoo!

23

The Sanctity of Life

December 23, 2001

Dear Praying Partner,

I hope this letter finds you well and enjoying the Christmas season, and I hope that you will enjoy all the blessings that God has in store for you today and every day.

I have been having the most difficult time writing this letter to you. Amidst the hustle and bustle of Christmas preparations, God's voice has been muffled, and I have determined that I do not want to ever write to you without hearing from him. You don't need to hear from me. I don't need you to hear from me. I believe that we both desire to hear God's voice, and I do believe that he speaks to us. And so, dear one, to that end I try to wait each month before writing to you.

The first three chapters of Genesis have been particularly important to me, as we are also preparing to celebrate the Sanctity of Human Life Sunday on January 20, 2002. This is the day that has been set apart to remember the anniversary of the United States Supreme Court decision to legalize abortion in the United States. It is a date and a decision that will live in infamy.

For about twenty years, Tom and I have been involved with friends and acquaintances around the world whose desire is to see the value of human life restored to God's original intent. We are created in his image. He gave us the command to be fruitful and to increase in numbers, and he gave us the charge to rule over the earth. Only about humanity did God say that we are created in his image. Only to humanity did he give the charge to rule over the earth and subdue it.

This morning I was so impressed by the question "How is God related to the processes of fertility?" In Genesis 1:22 he told the creatures of the sea and the air to "be fruitful and increase." In verse 28 he said to humanity, "Be fruitful and increase." God has never rescinded that command! That tells me that God thinks pretty highly of the human race. Shouldn't we do likewise?

Over the past twenty years, God has introduced us to some of the most amazing people—people of all ages, races, creeds, and social standings. These individuals are uniquely, wonderfully created in the image of their divine creator. Each one is dearly loved by him.

Last night Tom and I went to the John F. Kennedy Center for the Performing Arts here in Washington, DC, to hear Handel's *Messiah* as part of our Christmas celebration.

I cut my "musical teeth" on this glorious masterpiece, as my Dad taught it to me when I was young. I have heard it many times, but never before as I did last night. I am still overwhelmed by the power of God's Word so wondrously presented, and by his faithfulness to keep his Word.

Never before has Yeshua—the Messiah, the Anointed One—been more real and more precious to me. I am overwhelmed even now by what he has done for me—and for all of us—so that we might have an intimate love relationship with him. Just think: he loved us so much that he gave himself, his very own life, to save us from our sin, which separates us from him. Extraordinary!

Why is human life sanctified? Why should we value it? Why should we seek to protect and preserve it in any way? For one reason, and one reason only: because God does.

And so, dear one, please pray for me. Please pray for our team as we prepare for the Sanctity of Human Life Sunday: that God's message will be told, heard, and acted upon. He loves life! He loves people! Let us continue to do likewise, and let us continue to teach others to do so as well.

You are so very precious and so very dearly loved. God said so.

Because you live,

24

This Land Is Your Land

June 22, 2002

Dear Praying Partner,

She stood watching us as we drove through the gate. Her baby rested at her feet. I didn't see them at first, because I was so taken by the land and its mountain vista, and by the thought that this might be the land for which Tom and I had waited so long.

She was a cow, and at her feet was a newly born calf. At first the significance didn't dawn on me, but as I watched them, the symbolism grew and became unmistakable to me. That scene occurred on Monday, May 20, 2002. I'd like to tell you the whole story.

A number of years ago, some dear friends here in Washington started a group called the Brunch Bunch. At our first gathering, we were put into small groups and asked to discuss this question: "If I could have a monument built to myself, what would it look like?" I loved my friend Nancy's reply: "It would look like a huge chocolate fudge sundae with lots of whipped cream and a cherry on top." She has a great sense of humor.

Since I had never contemplated the idea of having a monument built to myself, I had to think about it. When it was my turn to share with the girls, I said that my monument would have women and children all over it! Little did I know then the significance of the question and its answer. Since then, my life has been enormously impacted by women and children, particularly widows and orphans—as I define those terms. And so, when I saw the cow and her calf and realized the gift that God was giving to us, I was deeply touched. As one friend put it, "This was one of God's vignettes of loving-kindness."

You see, on Friday, May 17, Tom and I had joined our friend Jim to look at a piece of property owned by his friend Scottie. Jim knows of our farm dream and the vision to care for women and children. That property had not been suitable, but Scottie had volunteered that he had another smaller piece if we would be interested in looking at it. We were, and we did. Oh, my! Was this the land God wanted us to have? We needed to think about it. Scottie said it was fine with him if we took the weekend to think it over.

We visited the land again on Sunday night and were even more taken with it than we had been on Friday. I kept thinking, "This land is your land, this land is my land ..."

Tom called Scottie that night and arranged a meeting for Monday morning. We decided to take one more look before meeting him. Once again, Jim accompanied us. Once again, we had the unmistakable feeling that this land was God's choice for us. After waiting and dreaming and hoping for so long, fifteen years or so, it was hard to believe that we were walking on such holy ground.

The land is beautiful—all twenty-six acres of it. It has woods, pasture, a beautiful mountain view, and a tiny stream. Our neighbor has horses, and a farmer is leasing the land now for his cows. You can hear the silence, the breeze, and the birds. It seems a perfect place for God to fulfill the vision he gave us so many years ago.

We are beginning to plan the buildings we will need, and the order in which they need to be built. We are so cognizant of our need for God's wisdom, direction, and provision, and we relish your prayers. And we look forward to your visits. We recognize that the land is God's land and that we are joining him in another glorious adventure. It is our desire that all that we do and all that we have will glorify him. Please pray for us to that end.

You are an integral part of this land and God's vision for it. Your faithful prayer support is a gift that has no price tag. We are truly grateful for you and your involvement with us. You are truly precious and so very dearly loved.

Love and hugs are flying your way,

Priscilla

PS: The farm has been blessed by many men, women, and children from all over the globe since its beginning in 2002.

25

His Ways

October 28, 2002

Dear Praying Partner,

As we approach Thanksgiving, I am truly filled with gratitude and joy. There is so much I want to tell you that I hardly know where to begin! So I'll just dive in, and let's see what happens!

October has been a very challenging month for me, providing me a number of chances to obey God's word to "give thanks in all circumstances," because that's what he wants me to do, even if I don't *feel* like doing it.

Tom and I were scheduled to clear the land for our first house on October 8, and we asked you to pray. On the evening of the seventh, we learned that there were problems with the bulldozer and the date had to be changed. This was not the end of the world, but it was disappointing. It was interesting, though, because only that morning we had visited the land with our pastor to pray over the land.

When he prayed for God's wisdom so that we would know exactly where to put the house, I thought it was a strange prayer because we had just told him that we had chosen the location. Well, we had staked out what we *thought* was the location!

Our pastor returned to Washington. Tom was unsure of the chosen location and wanted to redo what we had done. I was frustrated because this wasn't the first time we'd gone through the staking-out process. I had to go and be quiet and not try to force the answers to our questions.

Thank God that I could walk away and be still. Thank God that he wants to be involved in every decision that we make. Thank God that he sometimes prompts us to be still so we can experience him. Thank God that he speaks in still, quiet ways. Finally, Tom and I were able to choose what we think is just the right spot for our house.

We set up a second clearing date: October 25. I was excited because I thought I would have the chance to see the beautiful fall colors, which I love. But that wouldn't happen either. On the evening of Friday, the eighteenth, I fell through the storage room ceiling onto the concrete floor of the garage at the home of our daughter Emily and her husband, Tom. Miraculously, nothing was broken. I was just shaken up and bruised. Was I sore? You bet!

Over the next few days, I found myself getting depressed and irritable because I was focusing on the pain, whining, and indulging in self-pity. Finally, I realized what I was doing: I was being ugly. Ugh! Where was my gratitude that I had blacked out at the beginning of my fall so I didn't try to save myself and thus incur greater damage? Where was the gratitude that I have a loving family and friends who care about me enough to take care of me? Where was the gratitude to God for being the everlasting arms underneath me?

Surely an attitude change was in order. An attitude of gratitude was needed. The change performed wonders. I am grateful and happy to tell you that physically I am almost completely better. Emotionally

I am so much better. The Divine Physician is still on the job, and he makes house calls. Praise him.

And, dear heart, I am grateful for you. Thank you for your partnership in prayer, which opens so many doors to experience our wonderful Father. Please remember that you are a precious gift, and I thank God for you.

Finally, I am thankful that Abba has told us to give thanks in all circumstances. It may seem an odd thing for us to do, but Abba's ways are not man's ways. His ways are so much better, producing results far more wonderful than we could ever imagine. His ways are definitely worth doing.

Grateful hugs are flying your way,

Priscilla

26

The Message of the Babe

November 27, 2002

Dear Praying Partner,

Behold the Lamb of God,
Who takes away the sin of the world.
Oh, come let us adore Him.
Priscilla Flory

He was born in Bethlehem, the City of David: "This very day, in the town of David, there was born for you a Deliverer who is the Messiah, the Lord" (Luke 2:11).

He was heralded by the angel: "But the angel said to them, 'Don't be afraid, because I am here announcing to you Good News that will bring great joy to all the people'" (Luke 2:10).

He was visited by shepherds: "Hurrying off, they came and found Miryam and Yosef, and the baby lying in the feeding trough" (Luke 2:16).

He was announced by John the Baptist: "The next day, Yochanan saw Yeshua coming toward him and said, 'Look, God's lamb! The one who is taking away the sin of the world!'" (John 1:29).

As we enter the joy-filled Christmas season, let us come to the manger. Let us behold the beauty of the Babe, this Lamb of God. Let us bring him the gifts of our lives and our love, which are our acts of worship.

Always remember: you are so very precious and dearly loved. That's the message of the Babe.

Love,

Priscilla

27

In Due Time

April 23, 2003

Dear Praying Partner,

"Oh, no, not again!" was my response when I realized that Tom and I would need to delay the April date to move into our house. I must admit that I was disappointed, especially because our nineteen-month-old grandson was due to visit us while his folks took a little vacation. For months we'd all counted on our being settled in our new house on the farm.

The disappointment quickly changed to eager anticipation as I wondered what God wanted to do with us. A revision of our plans was quickly and easily accomplished. Instead of Lucas coming to us, we would go to him! It was immediately clear that God would work out everything for our good.

Do you remember the Rodgers and Hammerstein song, "Getting to Know You" from *The King and I*? It has been playing in my mind. Because of the delay in our move, I am having the joyful privilege of getting to know *my grandson*, who is a delightful and remarkable child. I would say that even if he weren't my grandson! He loves to go for walks, play in water, sing, dance, and play my pitch pipe. He loves to take pretend drives in the car and truck.

Lucas carries his beloved tool box everywhere. He is a social butterfly with a great imagination.

I am getting to know *our church family* at a nearby Baptist church where we have been warmly welcomed by the pastor and parishioners. They have made us feel at home with them.

I am getting to know *God*. He gave me the sweetest peace and eager anticipation about the delay. In fact, he has showered us with blessings that we would have missed without the delay. He has given me priceless treasures during this time with Lucas and the church family here. And because we were able to have a flexible schedule, we had a few days with Ashley and Greg, Lucas's parents.

In these times, when instant gratification battles patience, it has been good for me to learn to wait. The waiting has proved God's goodness, faithfulness, and wisdom. The delays have proved that everything does work out for good for those who love God and are called for his purposes.

I realize afresh that God makes all things beautiful in his time. Being on his agenda has been my greatest challenge and greatest joy. Patience is growing in my garden!

Abba frequently reminds me that the vision for the farm is *his vision*, and that he will bring it to pass. I must cease striving and let him be God. When I do that, dear one, the joy and peace that fill my heart are overwhelming, and all I can do is praise him.

And so the vision awaits its time. The move awaits its time. They will surely come. God has promised. What a day—a glorious day—that will be!

Loving you,

Priscilla

28

Dreams Come True

May 27, 2003

Dear Praying Partner,

Praise God from whom all blessings flow! We've *moved*! May 8 was the big day, and it was a beauty, filled with sunshine and a sprinkling of showers of blessings! Our dream is coming true, and Tom and I thank you for all your prayerful partnership. This new home is truly a gift from our Father above. We look forward to your visit.

As I sit amid the mountain of unopened boxes, I think of God's impeccable timing for our move. May 8 is the birthday of our beautiful daughter Emily, who has played a major role in our dream becoming a reality. She shares our dream and has worked diligently and given sacrificially to help bring it to pass. She makes her parents' hearts glad. And she makes her heavenly Father's heart glad as well.

As I sit here and enjoy the beauty of this tranquil place, I pray that all that we do here will gladden the heart of our heavenly Father. Will you join me in that prayer?

Oh, that you could see the wonders that our Abba has done. Rejoice in him and make his Father's heart glad.

He loves you, and so do I,

PS: Since our move to the farm, we have hosted family and friends from all over the USA, Argentina, Belarus, Egypt, Germany, Israel, South Africa, and Swaziland.

We have hosted seven weddings, our fiftieth wedding anniversary celebration, a funeral, numerous retreats, and other events.

I am grateful for each opportunity to share God's blessings to us with such priceless company.

29

The Dreamer

August 15, 2003

Dear Praying Partner,

"Baby, you must stop this moving from job to job. It doesn't look good on your resumé."

"Granddaddy, when I find the right thing, I'll stick with it." That conversation between me and my maternal grandfather Harry Buckingham took place forty years ago, and I will remember it forever!

Tom and I have known each other for forty-two years, and we have been married for thirty-eight years. I have been a mother for thirty-seven years. Tom and I have dreamed of having a farm for over twenty-five years. And the first prayer calendar was published fourteen years ago. I have always admired and respected longevity, a product of perseverance. The fact that someone has worked in the same job for many years has always impressed me. Long-term relationships impress me. The fact that Tom and I have known and loved each other for forty-two years amazes, delights, and yes, impresses me.

When Emily's older daughter, Lexy, was a baby, we used to laugh and say, "When Lexy is seven, we will move to the farm." On May 8, 2003, the day that Tom and I moved to our farm, Lexy was seven years and twenty days old!

What I realize is that God is in the midst of longevity, which is the product of perseverance, faithfulness, and patience. It is the product of his presence and his working in us. As I sit here and look at the beautiful place God has given to us, I am amazed and impressed with God's faithfulness, his patience, and his perseverance. He has a dream for us to fulfill, and he has patiently, lovingly been at work in us to bring it to pass. Because he encouraged me, I could keep going, even when I felt all alone. Because he was at work, I could trust that he would do what he said he would do, even when it looked impossible. Praise God! Because of his grace and faithfulness, we are living the dream!

And, dear one, it is my prayer that you will live the dream that God has for you in all its fullness. As you continue with him, may you experience the height, the depth, the breadth, and the length of his love for you. And may you love him with all of your heart and soul and mind and strength, for that is truly his dream for you.

Loving you,

Priscilla

30

Remembering Daddy

February 26, 2004

Dear Praying Partner,

The strife is o'er, the battle done,
The victory of life is won,
The song of triumph has begun,
Alleluia.
"Victory"

We sang this hymn at my grandmother Marguerite's funeral over forty years ago. She was a valiant lady who gallantly fought the physical ills that finally brought her down. I love this hymn because it speaks to me of her.

Last Thursday evening, my sister Harriett and I sang this hymn shortly after our father, Arold Ripperger, breathed his last. Daddy was a valiant man who bravely fought against the physical ills that finally brought him down. The hymn reminds me of Daddy.

Have you ever been with someone you love when they are in their last days? I had the opportunity of being with my mother and my father in their last days, and I found it to be an awesome privilege. Even though

I was not present when they took their last breath, I was able to be with them in their last days.

On the fourteenth of this month, Tom and I returned from a wonderful trip to Atlanta. Our granddaughter Megan had invited her granddad to join her for *Dads and Doughnuts* at her school. Megan wrote a biographical sketch of her granddad, and I was amazed to learn that Tom is ninety-nine years old and that his favorite TV program is football. We don't even have a television!

That same night we received a call from my sister Debbie, telling me that our dad had been hospitalized again. I could tell by the urgency in her voice that this time was unlike all the other times. Sunday morning found us at St. Joseph's Hospital in Baltimore. One look at Daddy raised a thousand thoughts, including, "How long, O Lord?"

The days that followed had an unreality about them, even though I knew that what was happening was real. By God's grace, there was a peace that disconnected me from the circumstances. I knew that we were waiting for the inevitable, and God granted me an amazing peace in facing that fact.

Family and friends came by to say farewells and to console and be consoled.

I think of my last days with Daddy, and I am grateful. I thank God for the opportunities to pray for Daddy and for the chance to release Daddy fully to his loving care. I thank God for the opportunity to encourage Daddy to go with Yeshua. I thank God for the reminder that the process was all about Daddy and what was best for him. I thank God for the chances to sing to Daddy, and I thank God for the precious gift of eulogizing him at his funeral.

I thank God for the gift of Daddy's life. It was a life filled with love—love for God, for his family and friends, and for the calling of God on his life.

Daddy spent his life in the service of God, leading men, women, and children into worship as an organist and choir director. As soon as I could hold a hymnal and read, I sang in Daddy's choirs. It was Daddy who first took me to church with him and introduced me to the family of God. It was Daddy who planted in me the love of worship for God.

The greatest thing he ever said to me was, "I pray for you every day." Knowing that he prayed for me daily gave me great peace. I am sure that even as he lay dying, he was praying for those he loved.

The greatest gift he ever gave me was the chance to be with him. It didn't matter what we did, whether it was playing, singing, praying, being quiet, or just being.

Daddy's death leaves a great void for all of us who loved him. Please pray especially for my stepmother, Eleanore. El valiantly fought on Daddy's behalf, when his physical problems made it impossible for him to fight for himself. It was she who made sure that he had the best of care, which she gave him herself. Her love and devotion to Daddy were beautiful to see in the everyday things she did for him. I think of this verse: "No one has greater love than a person who lays down his life for his friends." John 15:13 El was like that for Daddy.

Blessed be God, who gives us every good and every perfect gift. May you richly enjoy all the Father's blessings today and every day.

Love,

Priscilla

PS: On February 27, 2004, Mica Rose Bodkins, our youngest grandchild, was born. Life and death, the cycle of life, continues. Praise God for all his gifts.

31

Extravagant Gifts

March 20, 2004

Dear Praying Partner,

I remember. Christmas Day arrived, the family was gathered in the living room, and I was presented with two boxes. One was a huge one, and one was tiny.

I was given a choice: the big one or the little one. I could keep one, but I had to give the other one away. Which should I keep?

I opted for the huge one. It was a great choice, because it contained the most gorgeous full-length mink coat I had ever seen! I couldn't stop hugging it! Finally, between tears and laughter, I put it on. I felt like a queen. It has brought lots of joy over the many years I have had it. *It was an extravagant gift of love.* The tiny box contained chocolate-covered cherries: mmm, my favorites!

I remember. Another day, thousands of years ago, another gift was given. This one was a tiny living one, Yeshua, who would become a man and one day give his life to ransom the world. *His life was and is an extravagant gift of love.*

He was asked to give his life. For the joy that was set before him, he endured a cross. He hated the shame, but he did it anyway.

We have been praying that God would provide financially for the needs of our farm. I believe that God is asking me to sell my coat. I must tell you, dear one, that there are tears at the thought of giving it up. I love that coat and all it has signified of love and graciousness, of fun and laughter—not to mention that it served well in keeping me warm!

Its proceeds will be used to help build our chapel, and the joy of that is overwhelming. As I think of the opportunities that the chapel could provide for people to know Yeshua and draw closer to him, God's love and care overwhelm me.

We serve a risen Savior. He's in the world today. He loves us. He cares about us. He is intimate with us. He has plans for us that give us hope and abundant life. He invites us to give our lives to him. What a Savior!

Love and hugs are flying your way,

PS: I thought of *many* ways to sell the coat. Finally, my builder and I decided to trade the coat in exchange for his work on building the chapel. He was soon to be married, and the coat would be his wedding gift to his bride.

Tom and I were two of the few guests at the wedding. Seeing the look of delighted surprise on the bride's face when she saw the coat was priceless, and I cried tears of joy!

32

Hopes and Dreams

April 23, 2004

Hello, dear Praying Partner,

She stood still, watching us as Tom and I walked through the field. Her baby lay at her feet where she could protect it. I stood in awe, watching her. Spring has come to the farm, and with it the calving season.

Once again our field has become a maternity ward for our neighbor's cows and calves. Once again God demonstrates his amazing grace, this time in the birth process of the cows. As I watched this momma, I was reminded of the day that Tom and I bought our first piece of land. As we drove into the field May 15, 2003, a single momma cow and her newly born calf met us. Their memory is forever engraved on my mind. They were beautiful, just beautiful—a sign from God.

It is my hope and prayer that our farm will become a "maternity ward" for people as well as cattle. It is my hope that physical and spiritual babies will be birthed and grow here. I pray that God will birth dreams here and will draw people to himself as he fulfills those dreams. One of God's greatest gifts to me has been the fulfillment of dreams.

When I was a little girl I dreamed of being married and having children. Oh, my, how he has blessed me with Tom and our three beautiful children—David, Emily, and Ashley—and now even grandchildren.

I dreamed of being a missionary to Africa, and he has proved himself to be faithful in fulfilling that dream as well. It has been a great joy to tell others of God and his love for them as I have visited that continent and have had Africans live or visit with us.

I dreamed of having a farm where people could come and find rest, hope, and healing. He has given us the farm. Yes, it is still a work in progress, but he is in the midst of the progress, and I look forward to what he will do.

And, dear one, what about you? What dreams has Abba given you? It is my hope and prayer that as he fulfills your heart's desires you will experience him in new ways. I pray that he will give you a vision of himself and that you will draw closer to him than ever before. He loves you, and so do I.

Because he lives,

33

Listen!

May 24, 2004

Dear Praying Partner,

It is with great joy and gratitude that I write to you this month. Thank you for all your prayer support. Tom and I have been working on the plans for our new house, and *listen* seems to be our watchword. It comes up repeatedly so we can be on his agenda and not our own. Would he speak to us? How?

We thought we had the ideal plan for the house, but when the engineer sent the drawings back, we realized we were wrong! We prayed and asked for inspiration again. Once more we thought we had the right plan, only to realize that we had gone way over the budget! Now what? Tom said we should take a few days and listen for the Lord. That night before drifting off to dreamland, I asked God for some specific direction from his Word. Some solutions came to mind as I fell asleep.

The next morning Tom left to go on a trip for a few days. I decided to sit and be still. Perhaps God would speak. I felt impressed to continue our daily reading of the Psalms. Lo and behold, there was God's encouragement to keep on keeping on.

He has provided a house and a yard for us already, and we just need to keep on with plans for the new house. I shared our dilemma with Emily, and she immediately told me what she thought we should do. Later Ashley said the same thing. Hmm, it was exactly what I had thought of the night before. Perhaps, just perhaps, Abba was speaking!

When Tom came home, we redrew the plans, taking our daughters' advice. What was the result? What seems to be the best plan of all. Our builder was able to come immediately to collect the plans and deliver them to the engineer. We are now waiting to see the results of this latest attempt.

Thank you for praying for God's inspiration. You asked, and we believe we have received. I will keep you posted. To be continued …

One of my thoughts this morning was about God's faithfulness and his commitment to keeping his word. What he says he will do is exactly what he does. That kind of trustworthiness produces security and safety, because then we can know what we can do with him—and what we can't. We can know what actions we will provoke in him, because he has told us. God is truly a remarkable God and Father, the most wonderful parent who ever existed. Let us rejoice and be glad in him.

Because he lives,

34

Who Is Like Our God?

November 23, 2004

Dear Praying Partner,

We have been blessed by "The Best"! Heaven came down, and glory filled the earth! It is that wonderful time of the year, the time to remember God's wondrous blessing to us: that he came into the world as an infant, and the world has never been the same!

When you stop and think about it, isn't it amazing that a perfect and holy God would come to his creation gone astray from him? Isn't it amazing that he would take on our form and share in all the trials and tribulations that we experience? Isn't it amazing that he would take upon himself all the sin and cares of this world that we might have a new life in him? And yet that was exactly what he did, and he did it for each and every person who ever was and who ever will be—for all of creation.

Now he reigns in heaven and over the earth. He lives. Bless God, for we can say with Job, "I know that my Redeemer lives." How do I know? He lives in me. He lives in you. He said that if we would invite him to come into our hearts, he would come in and sup with us. I love the picture of God eating with us, making himself right at home in the center of our lives. Isn't that precious?

There are so many god "wannabes," so many idols and false gods that people have worshipped down through the ages—and still do today. They can't walk or talk. They can't interact with their worshippers. Food offered to them sits and rots until someone takes it away. They certainly can't save, heal, or give new life—or any life at all.

But our God reigns above all the earth. The sovereign ruler of heaven and earth reigns above every other so-called god. Yet he walks with us, and he talks with us. I spoke with him this morning. I was concerned about the fact that the insulation to be installed in our new house was to be the blown kind. Strange: we had never discussed that with our builder. However, after prayers Tom reminded me of the name of the insulating company, Awesome Insulation, a sign perhaps that God is in the midst even of insulation choices? Then I went to talk with the insulators and discovered that one of the ladies is a lovely sister in the Lord. I told her about my concerns and told her what Tom had said. She laughed and then calmly reassured me that all would be well.

Is there any god like our God? No, not one. Our God is the Kings of Kings. He is the LORD of LORDS. He is the ruler of heaven and earth, and he is the holy one of Israel.

May his blessings be yours now and always,

35

The Kaleidoscope of Faith

January 20, 2005

Regard it all as joy, my brothers, when you face various
kinds of temptation; for you know that the testing of your
trust produces perseverance.
James 1: 2, 3

Dear Praying Partner,

I have discovered that it's easy to read those words, and it's another thing to live them. Back in December I decided to read through the book of James every day for a week in preparation for a Bible study that I would start teaching in January. I was excited about the prospect of experiencing God and wondered how that would happen. However, I could not get past those three verses!

All through the fall, Tom had pains in his leg, hip, and shoulder, and we attributed them to maybe old age, perhaps a pulled muscle, or work on the farm. Finally, when the pains did not go away or even subside, Tom sought the advice of our physician. He made a few recommendations, which included Tom's seeing a urologist. Ultimately our doctor ordered a bone scan.

On Thursday, December 23, we received a call from him, and he informed us that he did not like what he saw on the scan. He wanted Tom to have a biopsy ASAP. We were in Florida with our son David, his family, and the rest of the clan to celebrate Christmas. The biopsy would need to wait until January. Merry Christmas!

It turns out that Tom has prostate cancer that has spread to the bones: stage 4 cancer. The prognosis: incurable. But procedures can be done to put it into remission. How do I count it all joy now? I looked at the part of the verse where it says "testing of your faith," and I looked at steadfastness, perfect and complete, lacking in nothing. Well, this certainly was a test!

It occurred to me that Abba wanted me to look at this situation from his perspective, and it would be very different from mine!

I love kaleidoscopes. I love all the different designs that you can make simply by changing the materials just a little bit. I decided to change my perspective. I decided to be grateful, and I decided to look forward once again to experiencing God. And I decided to give all of my burdens and cares to the LORD.

What a difference a day and an attitude change make! I decided to focus my attention on what I know about God. I realized that there are many things that I think I know, but there are two things that I am absolutely sure of: God is good all the time, and he loves us! That has given both Tom and me great peace in the midst of our storm.

We decided to go through the recommended procedures, and after the first treatment, Tom had absolutely no pain and was able to resume all activities, which he did with gusto.

We are not out of the woods, but we are experiencing God, and we are very grateful. We are grateful for all the love, prayers, visits, cards, and calls from family and friends. We are confident that no matter what happens, we are more than conquerors through Christ, who loved us and gave his life for us. We are peaceful because we know that God is in control and that he is able to keep us from falling, as his hands undergird us at all times.

Finally, we are experiencing joy. In fact, Abba reminded me of something funny in the wee hours of this morning, and I laughed so hard that the bed shook and I woke up Tom!

We firmly believe God's Word, which says that a merry heart does good like a good medicine. Why? Because we are experiencing it! There is so much more that I would like to be able to share with you, dear one, but time and space do not allow it.

In closing, I'd like to ask for your prayers for us as we continue in this process, and to thank you for your continued partnership in prayer. You are precious and dearly loved.

Hugs for the journey,

Priscilla

PS: As I write to you now, we are in the twelfth year, and Tom is looking good. The survival rate for men who have been diagnosed as Tom was—with stage 4 prostate cancer—is in the single digits. We continue to praise God for his amazing grace to us, as Tom has experienced every cutting-edge treatment for prostate cancer known to man.

We still think that gratitude and a cheerful heart are the best medicine.

36

What's It All About?

March 22, 2005

Dear Praying Partner,

Spring has sprung, oh, happy day! Winter is over, and the time of new life and rebirth is upon us. It is a beautiful day as I write to you. I can look out the window and see our new house awaiting our occupancy, because, you see, we did not move in last Saturday as we thought we would.

Last week, when Tom and I returned from our trip to Texas, which was wonderful, I felt so overwhelmed by everything that I couldn't begin to face all that a move would entail. So we decided to put off the move for one more week. And it's okay; it's really more than okay. *In his time, in his time, he makes all things beautiful, in his time.* We've waited for this house for over twenty-five years, so what are another few days?

I couldn't help but remember Tom's words: "Well, even if the house is finished in the winter, we'll probably wait 'til spring to move in." I had thought he must be joking! Hmm … this upcoming Saturday we will be in spring!

Thank you for praying for us while we traveled to Texas. I should have known that the trip would be a wonderful one, because it was difficult to do. I even debated about going. I couldn't get my act together to go because of a full-blown cold that wore me out, and because I had so much on my mind in thinking about our upcoming move. I finally decided to muddle through and go. After all, I decided, the trip was not about me. And, I thought, it was not a fashion show, so why was I so concerned about what I packed?

What was the trip about? It was about experiencing God. It was about experiencing God's strength when I felt too weak to hold up my head. It was about God's grace when I thought my eardrums would burst because of the pressure and congestion in my head. It was about experiencing his joy as we heard testimony after testimony of God's ability to heal and restore. It was about God's faithfulness to give me exactly what I needed when I needed it. It was about love: God's love expressed through dear old friends. It was about encouraging a brother and a sister.

Twenty-plus years ago at one of my favorite churches, the guest preacher spoke about mourning and how the church needs to learn how to deal with it. It was shortly thereafter that God began to teach me about mourning. I think of that preacher every time we do a Good Mourning conference. While I was in Dallas, I had the opportunity to tell him how God had used him. What a joy!

I trust that we will move into our new house on Saturday, and then we'll be busy getting it ready for you to come and visit. Until then …

Love and hugs are flying your way,

37

Hooray! Moving Day!

April 25, 2005

Dear Praying Partner,

Last month when I wrote to you, I closed with this: "I trust that we will move into our new house on Saturday." Well, trusting is being confident of what we hope for, convinced about things we do not see. Guess what! We did it! By the grace of God—and with the help of almost every member of our local church, prayer partners, and Dennis and the Stilwell family—we moved into our new house on Saturday, March 26, 2005! It was a most amazing happening.

The actual move began at 8:30 a.m. We were quite a picture with all our pickup trucks and Charles's flatbed. Some of the men loaded the trucks, some drove the trucks, and some unloaded them. They all moved so fast and so well that I had a hard time keeping up with them to direct where everything needed to be placed.

Some of the ladies stationed themselves at the new house, where they unpacked boxes and put away our belongings. Some stayed at the cottage and prepared lunch for everyone. By 11:45 everything we thought we wanted moved out of the cottage was moved out and into the new house.

At noon we all sat down to enjoy our first meal in our new home: lunch! After lunch our helpers moved on to other things, but not before thanking us for the opportunity to help! Can you believe it? They thanked us. Priceless!

The next week, prayer partner Loyonne came to help again. Later in the week, prayer partner Amy brought her three oldest children—Virginia, Zachary, and Joshua—and two of their friends to help. By March 31, when Ava and Isabella, our first grandchildren to visit, arrived, Tom and I were well settled and ready to have them.

We have now been here one month, and what a month it has been. Tom and I are grateful for the numerous opportunities we have had with family and friends. We are grateful for God's amazing grace and goodness to us, and we thank him for his gracious provision for us all. To God be the glory, great things he has done!

Love,

Priscilla

38

Dad

May 23, 2005

Dear Praying Partner,

Please pray with me:

"Our Papa, who is in heaven: your name is holy, sacred, and to be honored.

May your kingdom come. May your plans and purposes be done on earth just like they are in heaven, and let them begin with me.

Please feed us with your spiritual food to nourish our spirits, and feed us with physical food to nourish our bodies.

Forgive us for those things we have done that have offended you, and please forgive us for not doing what you asked of us.

Deliver us from temptation, and keep evil and the evil one away from us."

Thanks be to God for all that he will do in us, for us, and through us as we pray this prayer together. Thanks be to God for all the dads in our midst. May they richly experience the height, depth, breadth, and length of his great love for them. They are truly special people!

Because God loves you,

39

Life in the Kingdom

June 23, 2005

Dear Praying Partner,

I hope that this letter finds you well and enjoying the first days of summer. Here at the farm we have been enjoying the most beautiful days, which have ended with outstanding sunsets and evening skies.

Were you blessed in praying our version of the Lord's Prayer? I hope so! I certainly was. I would like to share one of the blessings that I received.

When I was a little girl and got hurt, my dad would say, "Come to me, and I will kiss it and make it better." Amazingly, it worked every time! On June 10, as I visited with Abba, he inspired the following:

"My Kiss Will Make It Better"

The words broke my heart that fateful day;
but as I listened I could hear my Father say,
"Come to Me my child,
and I will make it better."
The wounds were deep,
but I could hear my Father say,

"My kiss will wash the pain away.
I will kiss it and make it better."

Praise God!
His Word is faithful.
His Word is true.
I took my wounds to him. He kissed them.
They washed away.
His kiss has made me better.

Shortly thereafter, Abba took me through a beautiful healing time. His words of comfort and encouragement through this little poem were an essential part of the healing process. Yes, he reached down from heaven and brought his kingdom to earth, just as we asked him to do.

It is my constant hope and prayer that you will experience the height, the depth, the breadth, and the length of his great love for you, and that you will richly enjoy all the blessings he has in store for you every day. May his kingdom rule and reign in you forever.

Papa and I love you,

Priscilla

PS: As I read this letter eleven years later, I do not remember the pain or what caused it. I only remember that God took away the pain and the memory of the hurt.

40

Remember and Be Grateful

October 25, 2005

Bless *Adonai*, my soul,
And forget none of his benefits!
Psalm 103:2

Dear Praying Partner,

Remember. Remember. Remember. It's that time of year, once again, when we take special time to give thanks. I remember a friend once asked this question: "Who is the object of your gratitude?"

When he pointed out that our gratitude must have an object, I remember thinking, "What are you talking about? That's intuitively obvious to the most casual observer." But then I got to thinking about it. Who or what is the object of my gratitude? Why do Americans celebrate Thanksgiving? Who or what is the object of our gratitude? Are we even grateful?

The psalmist calls us to remember all the Lord's benefits and to bless him or make him smile. How can I make Abba smile? I can thank him!

This has been a remarkable year for us. We completed building our house (our fifth building) and moved into it with the help of our brothers and sisters from our church. It was a great blessing to see "the family" work so beautifully together, and we had fun in the process. When I remember all that we have been able to accomplish since we bought this land, I stand in awe of what God has done. *Thank you, Abba.*

We lived remarkably above the circumstances of cancer, and we experienced the reality that "a merry heart doeth good like a good medicine." I wish you could see how well Tom is doing. We believe that God has healed him and that he will keep the healing as well.

Throughout our long hot spell this summer, Tom worked diligently and completed our garage, worked in the garden, and built a picket fence around our pool—picket by picket. No ready-made fence for him! And we hiked a local mountain with our grands Lexy and Megan and our friend Robin. *Thank you, Abba.*

We traveled extensively, which was a surprise, especially the visit to South Africa. Our plan was to have our friends from around the world come to visit us, but we learned that Abba is a much better planner than we! *Thank you, Abba.*

Finally, he gave us you. Please know, dear one, that I do not take lightly the gift that you are. Your faithfulness to do the unseen work of prayer is greatly appreciated. Please know that through your prayers you are having more influence on our mission and in the world than you may ever know. Won't you join me in making Abba smile? *Thank you, Abba, for this precious one.*

Hugs,

Priscilla

41

Lemons Make Lemonade

Christmas morning, 2005

Dear Praying Partner,

Do you remember where you were on January 23, 1973? Do you remember what you were doing on that day? Do you know what happened on that day that would greatly impact our lives and the lives of many others?

I was a homemaker living in Annapolis, Maryland, at the time. We had three children, so I know I was doing something either with them or for them. At that time Tom and the children were my world, and I must admit that I was quite oblivious to what was going on in the rest of the world. Little did I know that the United States Supreme Court would decide that it is a woman's "right" to take the life of her unborn child, and that this decision would affect my life forever.

Today as I write to you, I am profoundly amazed at what has transpired over the last thirty-two years, particularly in 2005. Tom and I have continued to build the farm, completing our house, a pool, a garage, fences, and Tom's woodshop. We successfully battled Tom's cancer. We started a new business. We have been blessed by new relationships.

I can look down the hill and see the lights twinkling on the Christmas trees at the cottage. A new family moved in shortly before Thanksgiving. In a very short time, they have become dear to us, and we realize that their lives are a gift to us. In fact, all but a few of the presents under our tree came from them! I think giving must be their love language! They have a new puppy, and he adds his own personal touch to our lives. We look forward to getting to know all of them better—one day, one step at a time.

I am constantly amazed by our wonderful Abba. I love the way he can turn lemons into lemonade. The US Supreme Court's *Roe V. Wade* decision was truly a lemon, bringing incalculable harm, pain, and grief to countless numbers of people. Just think of all the people who are directly involved in each abortion. Yet God wants to turn every opportunity to choose to abort life into an opportunity to celebrate and choose life. He wants to bring healing and hope. He wants to bring life. That is why we have a farm. That is why we are building houses and barns. We want to be a place of *life*—abundant, Yeshua-filled, joy-filled, peace-filled *life* so that women can choose *life*.

Your partnership in prayer helps to make it all happen. Next year, 2006, has many new opportunities for us to experience Abba and to share his life with others. He came that we might have abundant life. Let's receive his gift, and then let's pass it on.

You are a gift, and I thank God whenever I think about you.

Most warmly,

Priscilla

42

More Lemonade

January 24, 2006

Dear Praying Partner,

We have a saying in our family: "Be flexible or be miserable!" Well, I can tell you this has been the month to practice flexibility! Would you like to know what happened?

First of all, thank you for praying for me when I was to be "on retreat" at the beginning of the month. The retreat was to be with some of my girl cousins, but the Wednesday before the big weekend gathering, we had to cancel for lack of participation! I was disappointed but thought I would look for God to bring something good out of the cancellation and disappointment. He does have his ways of turning lemons into lemonade!

Thursday night at our home group, I got violently sick. Things surely weren't looking good. On Friday I spent the day in bed with a great book, and I could begin to taste the lemonade! I was grateful for the opportunity to rest, and the book stimulated my thinking, which ultimately resulted in my drawing closer to Yeshua! He makes the best lemonade!

On the second Friday, I was invited by a former chaplain of one of our local correctional facilities to go to another correctional facility to visit some of the detainees we knew there. I was excited to go, because I hadn't seen them in almost a year. Four of us drove the ninety or so miles to get there.

Can you imagine our surprise when we were told that I couldn't visit our friends and that I had to wait out in the lobby by myself? I was stunned! But rules are rules, and my name wasn't on the list of approved visitors, so I had to follow the rules and wait outside.

I was overwhelmed by disappointment. Tearfully I watched the others leave. What in the world was I going to do for ninety minutes? The waiting room lobby was cold and uninviting. I hadn't even brought my Bible so I could have something helpful to read. I decided that I would pray.

My first thought was of God's ability to turn lemons into lemonade, so I prayed that he would turn this lemon into lemonade. I prayed for the team and the girls. I prayed for the authorities and the guards. We had a wonderful chat, God and I. I could begin to taste the lemonade. Mmm, so sweet.

At one point, a lady came in to start her shift. I heard her talking with the guards behind the glass shield. She told them she wasn't well, so I asked her if I could pray for her. She responded positively. I prayed that God would fill her from the tip of her head to the soles of her feet and that He would turn the lemons in her life into lemonade. I could tell that the Holy Spirit was touching her, so I kept my eyes closed so I wouldn't interfere with his ministry to her.

When we finished praying, she said, "Can I tell you something?"

"Sure," I said. Then she proceeded to tell me that she had visited her doctor that day. She had told him that she couldn't drink water. What do you think he told her to do? He said, "Then drink *lemonade*." You could have knocked me over with a feather! She went on to assume her duties, and I went back to my prayer bench.

Abba reminded me that St. Paul had sung while he was in prison, so it seemed like a good thing to do. I began tentatively, because I didn't know if the guards were paying any attention to me, and I didn't want to "make a show." But gradually I sang louder and louder. Abba was filling me with his own sweet brand of lemonade: praise!

Finally, the team returned. Bless their hearts, they were so concerned about me, but I was able to tell them of God's goodness to me. And then they regaled me with God's goodness that they experienced. Once again I experienced a flood of tears, but this time they were happy tears, tears of joy that our Abba is so good—so very, very good.

Dear one, are there some lemons in your life? Is there something going on that makes your lips pucker and your eyes squinch?

Be not afraid; be not dismayed. Our Abba would love to add his own sweetness and give you lemonade. Our dear friend and prayer partner Bill reminded me today that to get lemonade, the lemons must be squeezed. I don't know about you, but I don't like the discomfort of being squeezed. But I know this: when God is doing the squeezing, we can rest assured that the results will be wonderful.

So, dear heart, taste and see that the Lord is good.

Hugs for making lemonade.

Priscilla

43

Life in the Family

February 22, 2006

Dear Praying Partner,

It's going to be a beautiful day at the farm! Abba is in heaven and in his world.

It has been a great month, and I thank you for praying. We have much to be thankful for.

Our Bible study has been very rich and challenging. We have a wonderful group of ladies who love Yeshua and are dedicated to knowing and loving him more. Our teacher encourages us to live beyond ourselves in the love and power of the Holy Spirit, which is truly the only way to really live.

This year's National Prayer Breakfast was an unusual one for Tom and me, because we only attended part of it. We had been to every one since 1978. We went on Thursday afternoon purely to see friends. As we walked from the parking garage into the hotel, I asked Abba to guide our time and to give us his chosen appointments. Wow! We saw and visited with many of our prayer partners. What a gift to be with those we love, face-to-face.

On Friday Tom and I flew to Cancun, Mexico. We had some hilarious meetings, and through the week it was a wonder-filled time. To begin with, it was an all-expenses-paid trip, which we had earned through our new business. More than that, however, it was an opportunity to see and be with the people we work with. And what a great group they are!

On Sunday we had a worship service, which was very special because it included a time when leaders of the company made themselves available to pray for anyone who wanted prayer.

The next day a large group of us went to a village to visit the folks and to take nutrients for all of the children. Because of the generosity of our people and the company, all of the children will receive nutrient supplements for six months. I have to admit that I didn't want to come home when it was time, so you know it must have been a great time.

I just looked out the window, and it is snowing! You know, we don't have TV on the farm, so I don't usually know what the weather is predicted to be. The snow is a beautiful surprise. It's coming down softly and covering the earth. It reminds me of Abba's love: beautiful, pure, nourishing, covering the multitude of my sins, and making the world look beautifully different.

Dear one, isn't God good? Ah, yes, so good.

44

Because He Lives

March 21, 2006

Why are you looking for the living among the dead?
Luke 24:5

Dear Praying Partner,

He lives! He lives! Messiah Yeshua lives today! And because he lives:

- We can know eternal *life*, Yeshua himself.
- We can know that our sins are forgiven.
- We can know that our past is dealt with, our present is a gift, and our future is secure.
- We can know true love, the love that looks beyond the fault and sees the need.
- We can know true peace, the peace the world cannot give, the peace that allows us to forgive the most heinous grievances.
- We can be adopted into his family and experience the joy of brothers and sisters of all ages, races, and tongues. We can recognize and delight in our differences, knowing that our heavenly Father planned them.

Oh, dear one, we have a risen Savior. He wants to walk with us. He wants to talk with us. He has so much to tell us that we must know. Isn't it the most wonderful thought that the God who created everything we see and everything we cannot see wants to have a relationship with us? Isn't it wonderful that he wants us to join him in what he is doing throughout the world? Isn't it wonderful that he wants to live in us so we can fully enjoy him?

Oh, dear one, can you hear him? He's calling to you. Can you hear him? He says he loves you. Can you hear him? He says, "Come and see me." Have you seen how beautiful he is as he touches the untouchable? Have you seen his beauty as he loves the unlovable? Beautiful: he is beautiful. Do you see him?

As we celebrate his passion, his glorious resurrection, and his ascension, let us remember that he did it for love—love of the Father and love of humanity. Oh, dear one, what manner of love is this? It is wonderful.

Love and hugs are flying your way in celebration of our precious risen Savior.

45

Celebration Time!

August 26, 2006

Dear Praying Partner,

It is with a heart filled with gratitude that I write to you today. August has been a remarkable month for the "family." Thank you for all your prayers. God has visited his children. He has fought for them, and he has done great things for us all.

The month began with Tom's and my celebration of the day we met forty-five years ago. Ah, yes, we remember it well. Reflecting on the years we have had together, we can see that God has brought us a long way—a very long way—and that he has brought us all the way. I was particularly delighted that he inspired me to write a story called "The Diamonds."

The other day I received a fat envelope from Nepal. You can imagine my delight as a stack of handmade cards fell out of it. The cards were all made by the children at the orphanage in Nepal. I wish you could see them and the talent they display. These children will be the first to receive the vitamins in the Feed My Lambs project. Please continue to pray for them and all the children of Nepal.

The chapel is beginning to have walls and a beautiful colored-glass window. We have new fences and freshly cleaned-out areas where goats would be happy to live. I am finally seeing an end to the chaos that I call an office. Moving, battling cancer, and starting a new business took priority over organizing an office, but I must admit that I hate chaos. And it feels so good to have order in the place where I spend so much time.

Tom and I are grateful for all the blessings we have received through all who have come here to work, to play, or to find respite. To God be the glory, great things he has done.

Priscilla

PS: You may remember when we used to pray around the world for the children. We prayed for the children of Nepal when we started praying years ago for another orphanage in Nepal.

46

Heartbreak and Lollipops

September 25, 2006

Dear Praying Partner,

It is a beautiful autumn day here at the farm. The silence around us is beautiful, and a gentle breeze is blowing through the office window. With all this beauty, it is difficult to realize that the entire world is not experiencing what we are. For those who are hurting, for those who are hungry, for those who are lost apart from Yeshua—my heart aches. People wonder, "Where is God? Why doesn't he do something?"

I am reminded that his heart breaks for the same reasons mine does. Fortunately, he is actively engaged in his world to bring the comfort, strength, and hope that only he can.

Tom and I had the most wonderful time on our trip to Alaska, a trip we earned through our new business. We were bowled over by the beauty of the glaciers, the mountains, the fjords, and the people who were our cruising companions. Each day brought us a fresh glimpse of God—always a welcome sight!

Our trip started and ended in Vancouver, BC, Canada, where we were delighted to visit with our praying partner Edie, who is such a faithful lady—faithful to God and to her family and friends. We also had delightful visits with other longtime friends from golf and from our days in Washington, DC.

The settlement that I asked prayer for had to be done in two parts. The first part is done, and we are shouting, "Hallelujah!" I'd be dancing in the street if there was a street to dance in. God again proved his goodness and generosity, and for that I thank him!

I wish you could see the chapel! While we were away, Charlie, Robert, Raymond, Nathan, and Chad made great strides toward its completion. You know, it is an awesome thing to realize God's faithfulness. He planted the idea for the chapel in my heart probably twenty years ago. And now it is becoming a reality. Ah, yes, God is good, so very good. Is he faithful? Absolutely.

Remember: God loves you. Isn't that just the best news?

Hugs,

Priscilla

47

Little Things Mean a Lot

October 24, 2006

Dear Praying Partner,

Little things mean a lot. Good things come in small packages. It's the little things that count. One small step for mankind ...

Our Good Mourning "Day of Healing" absolutely amazed me. Our group was small—only eight of us—but God showed up. I'm so impressed by the fact that God cares about "small"—small groups, small tasks, and small people (as in children). Size really doesn't seem to matter to him. He will come and be just as real in a small group as in a large one.

The day was a beautiful one. As I sat quietly during my prayer time before the participants arrived, I realized that I had no clue about what Abba specifically wanted me to talk about, even though my cohostess and I had prepared lovely information packets. I had the sense that Abba was saying, "Don't worry. Just open your mouth, and I will fill it." Good idea!

I prayed that he would open my eyes to see him, open my ears to hear him, and grant me faith to believe him. I had a sense of how I thought the day should go. Well, I watched in amazement as he reorganized the day, almost moment by moment.

On October 16, my sister Harriett and her Nepali friend took off for seven weeks in Nepal. This would be his first visit home in ten years, and Harriett's first visit. We were all excited because they were carrying some very precious cargo for some very precious people.

In one of their suitcases they had one year's supply of vitamins for the fourteen children who live at an orphanage there. As we want to be able to provide these vitamins for five thousand children, fourteen seems a small number, but it's a start. It's a small number of children, but Abba loves each and every one of them as though they were the only person on earth.

These opportunities may seem small, but they have had enormous ramifications in my life already. Nothing is too small for God. Nothing is too big. He is the God of the impossible, and he is the God of the probable. He can do everything but fail.

Is there something in your life, dear one that seems too big for God? Is there something in your life that seems too small? Don't worry. Just hold out your heart and your hands to him, and then stand back and let him do his thing. You'll never regret it. You're more likely to be delightfully surprised at what God can do.

A small hug,

Priscilla

48

Looking Forward

December 28, 2006

Dear Praying Partner,

May the blessings of almighty God, our heavenly Father, be yours in 2007. May you experience the riches of his grace, the joy of his presence, the fellowship of his sufferings, and the power of the Holy Spirit to persevere in all things. And remember that in all things he works for the good of those who love him and are called according to his purposes!

Are you looking forward to 2007? Are you excited to see what Abba has in store for you? Are you eager to experience him and to grow in wisdom, knowledge, and love of him? I am. But I must tell you that there is a part of me that says, "Whoa, what if?" And my mind wants to focus on negativity. Can you relate? But I ask myself, "Has God ever failed you?" Just reflecting on our Christmas, I am reminded of God's faithfulness to fulfill so many dreams and desires that Tom and I had.

Remembering the darkest part of 2006, I am reminded that God was faithful to bring his light into my life and turn a most painful time into a reason to rejoice that our God is faithful.

Some 2007 opportunities that I hope for and desire your prayers for are these:

- to deliver the Sanctity of Life message at our church on January 21.
- to take possible trips to South Africa, Lesotho, Swaziland, and Haiti.
- to experience whatever surprises God wants to throw in!

Do you have any idea how precious you are? Do you have any idea how loved you are? Well, I can tell you that Yeshua stretched out his holy arms on the cross and said, "This is how much I love you!" Do you believe it?

Hugs for the New Year,

Priscilla

49

Widows of Antarctica?

January 24, 2007

Hello, dear one,

Many years ago, a dear friend said to me, "You can go anywhere in the world in your prayer closet." Do you remember when we prayed *around the world* by praying for the women and children by continent each month? Do you remember when we prayed for Antarctica? Did you think that maybe that was a little nutty? I did. Gracious! Aren't the only inhabitants of Antarctica penguins, seals, and polar bears? A lady asked me recently, "Why did you do that?" The answer is simple: Abba said to!

I would like to tell you a most wonderful answer to our prayers. At the beginning of this month, I was finally reading our Christmas mail. We received a letter from a friend out west, and in the letter a dear lady named Barbara wrote about her experiences with God in—guess where—Antarctica. No, I'm not kidding you.

And guess what else. Yes, she's a widow. I must tell you that this was a great faith-builder for me. And I have a new friend. We hoped that Barbara would be able to share some of her experiences with you in this letter, but the best laid plans of men do sometimes go awry. Isn't it wonderful that Abba's plans don't? Yes.

I know that he wants us to be encouraged that he speaks to us, even though sometimes what he says seems nutty to us. Take the other day, for example. I was impressed to read Luke 15:8. It made absolutely no sense to me at all. I read the surrounding verses and still saw no personal application. What did Abba want to say?

The next day I couldn't find my credit card—my "silver coins." I looked high and low, even under my bed. It was crazy. Finally, I remembered the last time I had used it: to buy gas for my car. I remembered the coat I had been wearing, so I went to check the pockets. Hooray! There was the credit card! Rejoice with me, won't you?

Yes, I'm glad I found the credit card, but more importantly, I'm glad that Abba speaks. I may not always understand immediately what he wants to say, but when I ask for wisdom and clarification, Abba is faithful to teach me.

Is he speaking to you? Does it seem wacky? Do you understand what he's trying to say to you? Do you need clarification? Ask him; he loves to explain. Why? Because he loves you!

Fear not; only trust him,

50

The Heart of the Father

February 16, 2007

Dear Praying Partner,

I am excited as I write to you this morning. Last night when I went to bed, I was so wound up by ideas and excitement that I couldn't sleep. Have you ever experienced that? I knew that I needed to get some sleep so I could function today. Because there were so many ideas from a number of people, I felt overwhelmed and confused about what to do with them all. My condition was not conducive to a restful sleep, and I need my sleep. I asked Yeshua to help. Peace was what I needed and desired. I asked, he gave, and I drifted off into a restful sleep.

This morning Tom and I sang a beautiful song about peace. It talks about the peace that only Yeshua can give. It's the kind of peace that allows us to live above the circumstances of life. The peace that he gives brings order out of chaos and results in joy. I remember when we were going through Tom's battle against cancer. I had Yeshua's peace, the peace that people don't understand, and with it there was an indescribable joy. In fact, one friend asked me if I understood the situation! Yes, I did. I knew that Tom had cancer, and the doctor had told us it was incurable. But I also knew that my God is bigger than cancer, and I told him so. Beloved, our God is bigger than any trauma. He longs to give us his order, his peace, and his presence.

Is there chaos in your life today, dear one? Are you feeling unsteady, unsure, unsettled? Do you lack peace? Have you asked Yeshua to give you his peace? Have you accepted the gift he wants to give you? His peace is a gift, and he offers it to all who will receive it.

Have you seen this slogan: "Know Yeshua, know peace. No Yeshua, no peace!"? It's true, you know. I've tried it both ways. How about you?

It gives me great peace to know that God loves me. Do you know that he loves you? Do you really know it? He does. He said so. He said that he loved the world so much that he gave his Son so that anyone who would believe in him would not die but have everlasting life. Now that's what I call love. That, dear one, is the heart of the Father.

Through all the years of praying, one thing is perfectly clear: the heart of the Father is love. It is a love that the world cannot give. It is a love that cannot be taken from you. It is a love so beautiful and so pure that there is nothing like it in the entire world. It is a gift to all who will believe it and receive it.

Thank you for going on this journey to the Father's heart with me. I hope that you have caught fresh glimpses of him. I hope that you have heard his words of love calling to you. I hope that you will respond to him with a resounding "I love you, Father." It will delight his father heart.

With love from the Father's heart,

51

Delightful Surprises

March 2, 2007

Dear Praying Partner,

Do you love to see the answers to your prayers? Do you love to hear what great things God has done? I do, and if you do too, then read on.

Do you remember that I asked for your prayers about any surprises that Abba might like to throw into our year? Well, he really surprised me in February, and the year has only begun! Oh, our Abba is such a delight. I am so excited about his surprises that I can hardly wait to tell you.

In 1990, when Tom and I went to South Africa for the first time, I met a lovely lady, Margaret Rundle, who has become a precious friend. In one of our conversations she suggested that I should write a book about my life. I thought that was a wonderful idea, and I wanted to do that. She became my "hound of heaven," asking me whenever we visited, "How's the book coming?" When her daughter Glenn suggested that I make a collection of our prayer letters, I thought it was a brilliant idea.

This morning I sat at my desk and held in my hands a copy of *Love Letters: My Journey to the Father's Heart*—my first book! Oh, dear one, I am overwhelmed by God's goodness to allow me the privilege of writing and publishing this collection of our years of journeying together in prayer. The tears of joy flooded my soul.

Writing the book was an experience that I will always remember with great joy and gratitude, because it gave me the opportunity to work with my brother-in-law, Denis, as my editor. You have prayed for Denis because he was in an auto accident with my sister Debbie back in September.

Reading over eighteen years of letters to choose just the right ones was a faith-building journey, as I was reminded of all that Abba has done in us, for us, and through us. It was a journey of love, and I can honestly tell you that I love God more than ever. I'm not quite sure what God's future plans are for the book, but one thing I know: if he doesn't do anything else with it, he has drawn me closer to him.

Other February surprises included a visit to Colorado to celebrate our granddaughter Mica Rose's third birthday. She is such a joy and quite the "princess" in the most delightful way. So it was only fitting that her party should have a princess theme. I wish you could have seen the bevy of princesses and princes who came to celebrate her life. Priceless!

The last surprise occurred on the last day of our trip to Colorado. In January I wrote to you about a lady, Barbara, whom I am getting to know, who lived on Antarctica. This past Tuesday I had the pleasure of meeting her face-to-face. Our mutual friend Steve invited us to his beautiful sanctuary in the midst of the San Isabel National Forest. As soon as I met her, I felt like I'd known Barbara all my life. Come to think of it, Abba had us planned from before the foundation of time, so I think we have known one another a long, long time! I look forward to getting to know her better.

As we continue through 2007, I hope that you will experience Abba's ability to surprise and delight. The prayers of the righteous do avail much, and I am grateful for your prayers. Thank you for your faithful partnership.

Hugs for continuing the journey,

52

Grateful to Go, Grateful to Return

May 5, 2007

Dear Praying Partner,

I went to Africa, hoping to be a blessing. My hope was to touch the children with the love of Yeshua. What do you think happened? Yes, they touched me.

Can you imagine sleeping with two other people in a bed and then having two bunks above you, each with three in them? Neither can I, but it is how some children live, and I was told that they are the *lucky* ones! They are blessed because Amelia cares enough for them to take them in and give them a place. The story of these children touches my heart, and I want to do something to change their situation.

Then there was the young mom with a month-old baby girl. I had the privilege of praying with them. The mom even let me, a stranger, hold her precious infant—a priceless moment. Then she looked me square in the eye and gently said, "One day I will send my daughter to you." Why? Only she knows, but her quiet and gentle way touched my heart. Perhaps one day Mandisa will come to visit.

In the space of twelve days, I visited four orphanages and one clinic and met loving, dedicated women who are doing monumental jobs in reaching out to children in need. Their love and dedicated service are beautiful to see. They touched me, and I will never be the same.

Thanks be to God for the precious team members who added their own brands of blessing to me and to the children and friends we visited.

Thanks be to God for the many friends we are privileged to have in Swaziland and South Africa, who added their own blessings. Thanks be to God for all who made the trip possible.

When I arrived at customs at Dulles Airport, the customs lady and I had a little bit of fun. Then she asked me what I had been doing in Africa. "Visiting orphans and friends, and encountering Yeshua," I replied.

She looked at me knowingly and said, "Welcome home."

Struggling through tears and the lump in my throat, I thanked her and said, "It's good to be home."

Grateful to go, grateful to return,

53

Simplify

June 1, 2007

Dear Praying Partner,

Simplify! Simplify! Simplify! This is my new marching order. It comes to me from the twelfth chapter of Hebrews, verses 1 and 2. This message has come to me three times now. The first time was Tuesday, here at the farm, in a prayer time with friends. The second was in our church Bible study on Wednesday night. And now it has come to me again as I asked the Holy Spirit to tell me what to write to you.

Simply said, Paul encouraged us to get rid of everything that keeps us from doing what Abba wants us to do. He wants us to keep persevering in running the race that God has for us: that's my race for me, and your race for you. I can't run your race, and you can't run mine. Paul encouraged us to keep looking to Yeshua, the one who planned our race and who will help us to complete it.

His race included a cross! He hated the shame of it. He dreaded the pain of it. But he did it! Why? For the joy that was set before him. And what was that joy? To be with the Father, in his rightful place.

So, dear one, I am trying to simplify. And that brings me to a very practical simplification: changing the way I send out this prayer letter.

I am a staunch traditionalist, and change doesn't always come easy. I love the idea of having a letter come in the mail, properly stamped, etc. You know what I mean. E-mail seems less "personal" somehow. However, I have decided (and as prayer partner Janice has said, "What took you so long?") to send out our letter through e-mail as much as possible.

I hope this process will help us to keep in touch—so we can keep in touch with our beloved heavenly Father, and so we can be a blessing to him and to those whom we seek to serve. Your partnership is a great gift, which I do not take lightly or for granted. Therefore, if you would like to stop receiving the letter, please say so. I certainly understand that as well.

Please remember that you are precious and dearly loved!

Hugs,

Priscilla

54

Little Girl, Arise!

February 1, 2008

> Now to him by his power working in us is able to do far beyond anything we can ask or imagine, to him be glory in the Messianic Community and in the Messiah Yeshua from generation to generation forever. Amen.
> —Ephesians 3:20, 21

Dear Praying Partner,

These words are appearing a bit fuzzy because of the tears that are rising. Fear not; they are tears of great gratitude and joy. The last few weeks have been emotionally packed, and yesterday was the climax of this amazing time.

When I was about eight years old, I learned about Africa for the first time. My teacher, Helen Coen, had a wonderful way of bringing geography to life. She taught my class about the Zulu people of South Africa. Little did I know then the impact that Helen's teaching would have on me, and the way Africa would become so important to me. Fortunately, God knew. After all, it was part of his plan for me.

Fast-forward to last fall when I needed to take some time to be still and to be quiet. It was then that God whispered, "The farm is in Swaziland." You see, Tom and I often talked of having a farm in Africa, only we thought it would be in South Africa. As only God can orchestrate things, the land for the farm is in Swaziland, but we can see into South Africa! Don't you just love it?

Tom and I immediately agreed that we needed to call Hixonia and tell her what we'd heard. She told us then that she had a farm under contract to buy. Would we be interested? Absolutely!

Hixonia sent us the information, and Tom and I decided that we needed to look at the property. Christmas Day saw our daughter Emily taking us to the Atlanta Airport to board a plane to fly to Swaziland.

As soon as we looked at the land, I knew it was God's choice for us. First of all, it is beautiful. The location is perfect, and the necessities such as water, electricity, and a hard-packed road are all there. More importantly, God's Holy Spirit was hovering over it.

There was only one problem: money. Where were we going to come up with the money needed to purchase it? And there was a definite time limit: January 31, 2008. Tom devised a payment plan, which we presented to the owners. They rejected it.

Much prayer covered the entire process. These are the prayers I remember specifically:

1. *Poppa, please give me a sign if this is the land you want us to have.* He did, and it was unmistakable, for only he knew what would touch my heart and give me his assurance.

2. *God, give us the best payment plan. I know that in your economy everyone is a winner.* Everyone got what they needed—the sellers, our real estate agent, and the buyer, Emmanuel Khayalethu Foundation.

3. *God, please multiply the $2.11 that Ava Grace gave me "for the poor children."* He has already multiplied it 47, 393.36 times! Now that's quite a return for an investment!

4. *Please multiply the exchange rate.* Not only did we get the land completely paid for, but the children got their school fees paid, the caregivers got their salaries, and there was money left for food.

5. *God, please give us wisdom.* He has given us a vision of what we can do and how we can participate in raising godly generations.

6. *Thy will be done.* I love God more than ever. Just to know him is to love him. And am I grateful? My heart is overflowing with gratitude! Yesterday, January 31, 2008, the land became that of the Emmanuel Khayalethu Foundation!

To God be the glory! He showed us that:

1. He has plans for us that are for good and not evil. He chose us to partner with Hixonia Nxumalo and the Emmanuel Khayalethu "family" to serve orphans in Swaziland. There are approximately 135,000 orphans in Swaziland.

2. He goes ahead of us and prepares our way. Obviously each step was thoughtfully set for us.

3. He is the greatest lover ever! He is passionate about children in general and orphans in particular.

4. He is faithful, faithful, faithful to his Word. In John 4:38 he said: "I sent you to reap what you have not worked for. Others have done the hard work, and you have reaped the benefits of their labor." When we returned home, we set in motion the mechanisms for the payment of funds to Emmanuel Khayalethu's foundation.

And we asked a very special friend to provide the funds so we could purchase the land. His response? "Of course I'll help. What do you need?" He sounded so like Jesus when he asked two of John's disciples, "What do you want?" Isn't it amazing that God cares enough to ask us what we want? And isn't it even more amazing that he will make the way for us to have it if it's what he knows is best for us? He is remarkable.

There is one thing I want. I want you to know the height, the depth, the breadth, and the length of his great love for you—and for you to respond to his call to you. Now that would complete my joy!

With great love and affection,

55

Why Wait?

August 29, 2009

Dear Praying Partner,

One of the greatest blessings of my time in Africa was the time I spent alone with Abba—to wait for him, to seek his plans for the day, and to give my time back to him so he could direct each day's path.

It has not been as easy to do this upon returning home, even though it should be. The difference, I think, is that here I know more of *needs*. I have a schedule, and I feel more in control. These can be great hindrances to what is truly important in the day. Yeshua told Marta that Miryam had chosen the better option in sitting at his feet to be with him and to listen. How much better a day goes, I've noticed, when I choose as Miryam did.

One precious thought came from my time of waiting this morning: my mother's birthday is in September. I thought of my mom and was so grateful for her. She gave me life, and she sacrificed often for me and our family. Though small in stature, she was a great lady. I am eternally grateful for the gift of her life.

I am also grateful for the many ladies who will experience the labor of childbirth this month. We will continue our tradition of praying for those women who will be in labor on "Labor Day." May they and their babes experience God in their labors.

When I was in Swaziland I heard a lady say that children are the future of any nation. I immediately disagreed with her. Why? Because children are our present. They are God's gift to us *now*. They know and experience the same Yeshua, the same Holy Spirit, and the same heavenly Father we do. The Holy Spirit is just as active in children as he is in adults. Furthermore, we are only guaranteed the present moment, and that is a great gift!

Oh, dear one, our Abba is so good and so great. How can we do anything but love him? He is calling us to be with him. Out of our being will come our doing. With the being will come the peace, the joy, the clarity, and the strength for the doing. We may do less but accomplish more.

Hugs, love, joy, and peace to you as you wait,

56

Build It, and They Will Come

May 25, 2010

"If I raise my eyes to the hills,
from where will my help come?
My help comes from ADONAI,
The maker of heaven and earth."
Psalm 121:1,2

Dear Praying Partner,

One of the joys of living here at Providence Farm is waking up and seeing the beautiful Blue Ridge Mountains. As I write to you now, the view is clouded over, and the mountains are only faintly visible.

I often think about how the mountains remind me of God. Like the mountains, he is rock solid and always near. He is immovable and unshakable. Sometimes he is clearly visible, at other times he is completely hidden, and at still other times he appears to be in a mist. This month he has seemed to be all of those things. It has been *one of those months.*

On May 1 we celebrated our first wedding here at the farm. John and Pat were *officially* united as husband and wife in a very lovely ceremony celebrated by their families. I remember Tom's asking me during the planning stages of building the chapel why we were making the chapel so big and what we would use it for? I wasn't clear about the specifics myself, so I couldn't give him a clear answer. I just knew that if we built it, Abba would use it. Clearly, on May first, Abba was in our midst and smiling!

Praise God for the gift of marriage and family, two of his most brilliant ideas!

Pray that John and Pat will draw closer to each other as they draw near to God.

On Sunday Ashley, Lucas, Mica Rose, and I went to look at a litter of Lab puppies. Clearly, one of the pups would be going to Massachusetts with them when they went home! Tux was chosen and is doing well in his new family home!

Praise God for the gift of pets to love and care for.

On May 16 we celebrated our first memorial service in the chapel. In January our new friend Susan succumbed to cancer. Before she died, she visited the farm and was so taken with it and the chapel that she asked if she could have her memorial service here. Absolutely.

As you well know, the winter weather didn't cooperate, so the service had to be put on hold. As we all know, Abba's time is always perfect, even if his reasons aren't clear. But once again it was clear that he faithfully showed up and blessed us, one and all.

Praise God for Susan's life, her family, and her friends.

Pray for Abba's comfort for her children and their spouses and children.

Yesterday we couldn't see the mountains because of the clouds covering them. Abba seemed just as invisible, as dark clouds of confusion and discouragement filled my heart and mind. Last night Tom and I were scheduled to talk with some folks about providing our nutritional products for children in Uganda. I was so excited by the prospect. Obviously the Enemy's forces weren't so excited for us, as they were making life very difficult, to say the least!

Finally, it dawned on me what was happening, and I mentioned to Tom that I knew God must have something wonderful planned for us that evening. I decided to speak and obey the Word of God:

> "Therefore, submit to God. Moreover, take a stand against the Adversary, and he will flee from you."
> James 4:7

As I repeated God's Word over and over in my mind, the clouds lifted, and the peace of God returned. We went to meet the folks and had the most wonderful time with them.

Praise God for the gift of brothers and sisters who are like-minded and share a common goal.

Praise God that when Emily, Lexy, Megan, and I go to Swaziland, we will be able to take a three-months supply of nutrients for two children's homes.

Pray that we will be able to continue to provide the nutrients for the children and staffs, and that they might enjoy improved health.

Please be in prayer for our Good Mourning mini retreat on June 12 from ten a.m. to four p.m. I am so excited about the team that Abba has put together to host and carry out the day. I know that he has a perfect guest list, and it will be a joy to see who comes. You, of course, are most welcome!

Please remember the widows and orphans of Eastern Europe, especially those in Belarus at Hope Home.

Thank you for being the precious part of my life and *family* that you are. I thank God for the gift of you, and for the service of prayer that you provide. I pray that as you seek him you will find him, and that you will enjoy the love, joy, hope, and peace that only he can give.

You are priceless!

Priscilla

PS: On my last trip to Belarus in 2012, I visited Hope Home and was delighted to learn that it has become a model home, showing others how to care for children who are physically challenged—some of whom are even in hospice. The loving care that the children were shown was inspiring.

57

Exercise Your Prerogative

June 29, 2010

> But to as many as did receive him, to those who put their trust in his person and power, he gave the right to become children of God, not because of bloodline, physical impulse or human intention, but because of God.
> John 1:12-14

Hello, dear Praying Partner,

Last Saturday a group of ladies gathered here at Providence Farm to have an afternoon of relaxation and refreshment. Our theme for our time together was "Exercise Your Prerogative." In thinking about what that meant and what the Holy Spirit wanted to say, I was rather overwhelmed by the prerogatives we have as children of God by his amazing love and grace.

First and foremost, we have the right to become His children. Think about it! The awesome God, creator of the universe—of everything we see and can't see—gives you and me the right to become his children. And think about this: we have a Father in heaven who loves us more than life itself. After all, he gave his life so that we might live.

Second, we have promises that are uniquely for his children. We have unlimited access to his presence. He promises he will never leave us, forsake us, or reject us. Is that heavenly? Yes.

He has plans for us that are for our good, plans that include his guidance and partnership—if we will exercise our prerogative and ask how we can fit into them.

And—glory, hallelujah! —he has a home waiting for us that will far surpass anything we have here on earth. He will be there, and we will see him as he truly is.

In April I asked you to pray for our friend Richie because he had a brain tumor. He is now at home with Yeshua. We praise God for the gift of his life and friendship, and for the knowledge that he is now at peace.

It is a great joy to have the right/privilege/prerogative to extend hospitality to our family and friends and to enjoy together the greatness of our God and Father. We have joy, such joy.

Once again we were privileged to host a day of Good Mourning. About thirty folks, ladies and gentlemen, gathered here at the farm to explore what Abba has to say about mourning, to worship him, and to give him the freedom to work in our lives. It was a great joy to see people set free of pain from their past, to see them experience the love of God through his forgiveness and amazing grace. I wept with joy through most of the memorial service. The testimonies we heard throughout the day touched deep places in our hearts as Abba poured out the balm of Gilead.

It has been a beautiful month, and I thank you for your prayer support. I know that we cannot live without it.

This weekend our family is gathering to celebrate the birth of our great nation. I am so excited, because this is one of my favorite holidays. While I was growing up, it was always a special time for our family.

My maternal grandmother was born on July 4, and I always thought of her as our little firecracker. She was quite something.

On July 12, Emily, Lexy, Megan, and I leave for Swaziland and will return on July 28. I am so excited to have this opportunity to be with my daughter and granddaughters on this grand adventure. I am eager to see what Abba will do with us.

Please pray for us regarding these concerns:

1. Pray for safe travel. Pray that we will be on God's agenda, that we will have favor wherever we go and with those we meet, that we will have holy boldness to declare the gospel as we should, and that Abba will open doors for us that we could never open ourselves.

Emily and I decided to fast and pray each Monday, especially for Emmanuel Khayalethu (EMK) and for other needs as God presents them. You are cordially invited to join us wherever you are. How you fast is totally up to you. I always remember one friend who fasted from saying negative words. She was amazed at how that changed her life. We are already seeing God answer our prayers, and for that we rejoice and thank him.

2. EMK needs twelve dining tables and forty-eight chairs. We have a man who can make them for $3,000. Salaries for the staff are an ongoing need of $5,000 monthly. We are working on building a recurring, sustainable income for EMK.

3. Please mark your calendars and pray for these upcoming events:
   Mondays: prayer and fasting
   Saturday, October 16: for people to come and hear from Tass Saada, author of *Once an Arafat Man*. Tass has a remarkable testimony of Yeshua's love and grace, and you will be blessed to hear him.
   Saturday, November 13: Good Mourning session. Gentlemen, this is not only for ladies. You are cordially invited.

July 10, 2010

And here's more.

Thank you so much for your prayer support! I hope that you survived the heat wave of the past week and are enjoying the warmth of Abba's love!

It was a great joy to have our children, grandchildren, a niece, a cousin, friends, and neighbors gathered to celebrate the Fourth of July. The house overflowed with joy and laughter. Safe travel was experienced by all as they travelled to and fro. Praise God.

As we know, God works all things together for those who love God and who are called according to his plans. For many months now I have asked you to pray for my cousin Phyllis and the health challenges she has faced. She now has a challenge of another kind. By God's grace, she is seeing his loving hand in her life. She's amazing.

She returned home from the farm on Monday, and on Wednesday morning in the wee hours, she and my uncle were rudely awakened by the sounds of explosions. He woke to see flames outside his second-story bedroom window, and in no time the house was destroyed by fire.

Praise God that they were miraculously unharmed! Praise God for their faith that God is a loving Father. Please pray for them as they make the many adjustments that are required because of the fire.

Our praying partners *Audrey* and *Julia* are living with Parkinson's disease. Praise God for these precious ladies' faith in a loving, sustaining God. Pray that they will experience his love, joy, and peace as they continue their walks of faith. May he give them wisdom, knowledge, and discernment daily that they might overcome this unfriendly visitor called Parkinson's.

It is my hope and prayer that you will richly enjoy all the blessings that our heavenly Abba has in store for you. *You* are his child, and he loves you more than life itself. Exercise your prerogatives, and call on him. Enjoy his presence, experience his love and grace, and know that he is God!

Hugs for exercising your prerogative!

Priscilla

PS: As I write to you now, these precious ladies—Audrey, Julia, and Phyllis—are exercising their prerogatives and enjoying heaven.

58

The Hope of Heaven

December 31, 2010

But for now, three things last-
trust, hope, love;
and the greatest of these is love.
1 Corinthians 13:13

Dear Praying Partner,

"Hello, Mr. and Mrs. Flory, this is Dr. Whitworth." Tom and I had been waiting for this call, which came shortly before Christmas. We knew that the news he had for us would significantly impact our lives, but we felt very prepared for what we believed he would tell us: "The cancer has returned, and you will need to undergo treatment."

Perhaps you remember that in January of 2005 Tom was diagnosed with metastasized prostate cancer. By God's amazing grace and infinitely creative genius, he took away the cancer, and Tom has been cancer free. Every six months Tom went for checkups, and each time he was still cancer free—until eighteen months ago when the test results showed little signs that the cancer had returned. His last test had showed enough marked activity that Dr. Whitworth had ordered a bone scan, which would be the definitive test. "Don't make any plans until the test results are in" was his recommendation. Hmm, so what would happen to the plans we had already made?

Not wanting to cause alarm we decided to keep this information to ourselves. This was extremely difficult for me at first, because I always want to get everyone I know to pray. However, for this time and this issue, it would be kept among God, Tom, and me.

We had traveled the cancer road before, and we prepared to travel it again. We had wonderful talks about many things, including our relationship, where we are both still number two in each other's lives. We discussed the big "what if" question as we contemplated the possibility of Tom's death, and we shared thoughts of heaven. We had the opportunity to test our faith in Paul's words to the Philippians: "For to me, life is the Messiah, and death is gain." Philippians 1:21 Did we truly believe that? We did. We truly got excited by thoughts of heaven and what it is like, and the reality that Yeshua is the hope of heaven. To be with him forever—oh, glorious thought!

The time of waiting—from the visit to Dr. Whitworth, through the bone scan, to hearing the results—was a time of amazing grace. God gave us peace: whatever the outcome, Abba would be with us. He gave us joy in just being together and enjoying the simplicities of life together. And he gave us work to do: a trip to New York City to pray at Ground Zero and at the site of the proposed Islamic mosque.

Finally, the call came: "Mr. and Mrs. Flory, this is Dr. Whitworth, and we have the results of the bone scan. I think you're going to like them." His voice on our message machine was excited, so we called him immediately. But we had to wait a little longer, because we didn't get to talk to him until the next day.

When we finally talked with him, the news was truly amazing: once again, there was *no sign at all of the cancer.* We were so excited that we could hardly stand ourselves. It seems that Philippians 1:22 was a message for Tom as well: "But if by living on in the body I can do fruitful work, then I don't know which to choose." Philippians 1:22 So, we continue to seek the Father's will, his grace and wisdom, and his plans for our lives so that we might be fruitful in his kingdom.

This year Christmas had a whole new meaning for me, as I had been given the two most wonderful of gifts. There was the gift of my beloved husband Tom being in good health, and the renewed sense of wonder that each and every minute is a gift from God to be lived to its fullest, to be appreciated and enjoyed. The second gift, which is truly the most amazing, is the gift of Yeshua, "the hope of heaven." He is our blessed hope, and all who hope in him will delight him and experience his unfailing love.

Can you believe the amazing truth that God came to earth so we could know him intimately and experience his amazing, unfailing love? That is our message of hope. Yeshua, Hope of Heaven, came to earth so we can have the hope of heaven where he reigns and where there will be no more sorrow, sin, or death. Until that day when he calls us home, we will hold on to his glorious hand, knowing that with each step he will draw us closer to our glorious hope.

I thank God also for the gift of you, dear one, and I hope and pray that you will experience the richness of "Christ in you, the hope of glory." You are truly precious and so dearly loved. Abba said so, and Yeshua came to earth to show you!

Love and hugs are flying your way,

59

Hear the Lion Roar

May 7, 2011

Stay sober, stay alert! Your enemy the Adversary
stalks around like a roaring lion looking for
someone to devour.
—1 Peter 5:8

One of the elders said to me, "Don't cry. Look, the Lion
of the Tribe of Y'hudah, the Root of David, has won the
right to open the scroll and its seven seals."
—Revelation 5:5

Dear Praying Partner,

I am amazed at God's timing! I am keenly aware that this April has two significant events: April 15, when our US income taxes are due, and April 24, the celebration of the resurrection of Yeshua of Nazareth! And I have to make an accounting for all of our Africa trip finances (a third occurrence), which has meaning for me but is of no significance to anyone else!

On March 31 Tom and I returned from a ten-week visit to Africa. It was a most wonderful trip, and there are many stories to tell, but the one I want to share happened yesterday. I encountered real, live lions!

I hope and pray that this story will encourage you and draw you close to the Father's heart.

It is my job to handle the finances for our trips, and that includes making an accounting for our expenses. Having been gone two and a half months, they were many. Tom and I had collected all the required receipts and did a lot of the work together, but the final preparation fell to me. I was overwhelmed by the prospect, and my stomach began to knot up.

I grumbled and began to do my job with lots of grim determination and fear—and certainly no joy or gratitude. Little did I know the wonders that Abba had in store for me in the process.

"Fears? Did you say *fears*?" you might ask me.

Yes, I said *fears*.

"Why were you afraid?" you ask.

Simply put, the devil, roaring around like a prowling lion, wanted to destroy me, and fear was his weapon of choice. Blinded by these fears, I didn't realize how groundless they were or how much I was controlled by them. Where was the self-control? Where was the faith?

You see, when I was in the ninth grade, my dad, who was a lawyer and our church worship leader, was sent to prison for income tax evasion. At the time, I didn't think it affected me, even though someone made a smart aleck remark about it. But an arrow had been launched and pierced my soul: the *fear* that I too might be sent to jail if I wasn't careful! That fear would raise its ugly head often, many years later, as I began to take people on trips to Africa and was responsible for the finances. But God, our God, the Lion of the tribe of Judah, would conquer that fear and defeat the devil, who wanted to destroy me.

This is what happened. As I was preparing my accounting, I had to ask our accountant a number of questions, which she graciously answered, being very patient with me. I kept asking about one particular line item, which she explained repeatedly, until finally she said, "Priscilla, that's how it is, and I don't know any other way to tell you." It wasn't that I disbelieved her; it was just that the answer was so surprising to me that I could hardly believe it!

Finally, I began to understand. Finally, it all began to make sense, and I realized the wonders of our gracious God. He was showing me my fear of going to jail for improperly accounting to the IRS for my finances. I also feared what people would think. He began to show me that these fears were the cause of anxiety that ultimately resulted in the sickness I always got when I thought about trip finances.

Then he showed me that this accounting, this accountability, this process that I dreaded, was his protection for me. Our wonderfully knowledgeable accountants were my shield of protection. They would not allow me to do anything illegal or immoral. If I made mistakes, they would correct me.

I began to feel Abba's amazing love and grace as he took away my fears and filled me with quiet confidence in him and the people he has placed in my life.

What a change! What a difference *truth* makes! The freedom is fantastic. I can honestly say that I am thankful that I have encountered the *lions*.

The devil is crafty. Like a lion, he sneaks up on his prey and pounces, sinking his teeth into the heart. Oh, he is strong, and he can kill. But the Lion of Judah is stronger. He is mightier and wiser. He is motivated by love, not hate. He is motivated by life, not death. After all, that's why he came to earth. He loved us so much that he gave his life so that we might live. And it wasn't just so we could exist or survive, but rather that we might have abundant life and *thrive*!

Although I have been close to a lion in the wild in Africa, I have never heard one roar. I imagine that the sound can be pretty scary. Our enemy, the devil, roars, and he can be pretty scary. But I love it when the Lion of the tribe of Judah roars! He is alive and roaring: "I love you! You are precious, and I love you!" Can you hear him?

Please pray with me:

> Dear heavenly Father,
>
> There are many in our world today who need to hear your roar. They hear the devil far too much, and they need to hear you instead. We pray especially for the children of the world whose parents are incarcerated and who may be fearful. You know their hearts, and you know their needs.
>
> Please set them free so that they will follow in your footsteps and experience all the love, joy, and peace you have and want for them. Quiet the roar of the Enemy so that your voice will be heard, your Word will be believed, and your purposes will be accomplished in them, for them, and through them.
>
> We are grateful that we can come to you at all times, in all places, for all things. Thank you that you do so much more than we could ever dream of or ask for. We love you.
>
> Gratefully, amen!

Until I see you, love and hugs are flying your way,

60

A Diet for 2012

January 30, 2012

Hello, dear Magnificent One,

Here we are at the end of January, and I am already wondering, *where has the year gone?* January has been a great month. It's not always easy, but sometimes the more difficult times are the best times.

Prayer has been a theme for the month, and I would like to invite you to join me in praying for each other and for our work in The Family Extended.

For our first letter of the year, I am including a letter I wrote at the beginning of the month. I hope you will be encouraged as you read it.

> Dear Ladies,
>
> When we were together recently, we talked about *dieting*. I suggested that we might want to pray for each other. This morning my mind was drawn back to our conversation, and I would like to share some of my thoughts with you. Do with them as you please.
>
> First, I thought of a song we all know, "Seek Ye First," where we are told that we should seek God's kingdom and

his righteousness above all things. Man needs more than physical food; there is life in the Word of God. This seems an appropriate theme song for 2012.

Then I thought of the word *diet*, and the following acrostic came to mind:

D = *Devotion*. May our devotion be to Yeshua, to love him with all of our hearts, souls, minds, and strength. Like the wise men of old, may we be devoted to seeking the King.

I = *Inspiration*. Let us breathe in the fresh air of the Holy Spirit to have his infilling of wisdom and delight.

E = *Encouragement*. Let us encourage ourselves and each other and let the Holy Spirit encourage us as well. Life is not always easy, and we sometimes get discouraged. Sometimes we need to do as the psalmist David did. He said, "My soul, why are you so downcast? Why are you groaning inside me? Hope in God, since I will praise him again for the salvation that comes from his presence" (Psalm 42:5). Sometimes only God comforts us.

T = *Trust*. "Trust in *Adonai* with all your heart; do not rely on your own understanding; In all your ways acknowledge him; then he will level your paths" (Proverbs 3:5–6).

I have thought much about the wise men who visited Yeshua. They saw his star in the east, and they came to worship him. They were devoted to finding the King, and when they had found him, they worshipped him. As we, each in our own way, seek the King, it is my confidence and prayer that we will find him. It is also my prayer that we might experience the height, the depth, the breadth, and the length of his great love for the world. And may we, like the wise men of old, worship him.

May you richly enjoy your 2012 diet!

Priscilla

Thank you for allowing me to share these thoughts with you. May your 2012 be filled to overflowing with the bounties of Abba: love, joy, and peace.

Prayerfully yours,

Priscilla

61

The Eagles Have Landed

January 13, 2013

Dear Magnificent Sevens,

It is with joy and gratitude that I write to let you know that the *eagles, Tom and Priscilla,* have landed in Johannesburg and are planning to leave for Swaziland on Monday morning. The flight over was easy, and we were easily ensconced in our hotel in Joburg.

Saturday provided a few surprises, as Tom and I spent the day with our Willow Run partners, Lorrie and Dewey. At breakfast we spent time with Henry, Jack, and Steve, who departed Washington today for Uganda. Tom and I plan to visit Uganda in February to celebrate the university graduation of our dear young friend John. John plans to start a school, and Abba has been showing his support.

We also hope to visit our friend Anne while there. We met Anne years ago and are eager to see her and the home she started for street children.

We have planned a two-week visit to South Africa, starting January 20.

We have learned to hold on to our plans loosely. We want to make room for the moving of Holy Spirit, even though our desire all along has been to be on *his* page.

Saturday at breakfast, Jack asked if we had an agenda for our trip. He smiled and winked as he said it. I promptly replied, "Yes, as a matter of fact, we do have an agenda." And then I shared it with all who were breakfasting with us.

Here it is:

1. Devote ourselves to prayer, being watchful and thankful
2. Pray that God will open doors for us so that we may proclaim the mystery of Yeshua
3. Pray that we might proclaim it clearly and boldly
4. Be wise in the way we act toward *outsiders*
5. Make the most of every opportunity we have
6. Let our conversation be always full of grace, seasoned with salt, so that we might know how to answer everyone.

I hate to have to admit it, but at the Dulles airport I failed miserably at numbers 5 and 6 when I gave in to anger at the TSA agent who confiscated some of my brand new Ahava products. I had totally forgotten that they were in the wrong suitcase. He caught them, and I paid the price. Ugh!

However, I was reminded that Abba is the God who forgives, and I am not perfect and therefore stand in need daily of his amazing grace.

My hope is that I will do better each day and exalt Yeshua and not drag him down.

Please pray for us as we journey on, that we will witness to Yeshua and bring him glory as we ought to do.

You are priceless and dearly loved. Abba mentioned that first, and I heartily concur.

Here comes a *big* hug,

Priscilla

62

From the Ends of the Earth

Friday, April 5, 2013

Altitude: 36,025 feet
Land speed: 408 mph
Time: 3:30-ish

Dear Magnificent One,

We—I and my fellow travelers aboard South African Air, flight 207 from Johannesburg—are high above the earth, speeding on our way to Washington's Dulles Airport. Many will continue on. Tom and I, Tony, Jennifer, Samantha, and Anthony Hayes still have a way to go to reach our final destinations: home.

Each person on this plane has a story to tell. This is my story!

Leaving home in January, I could never have guessed or planned all that would take place between then and now. Nor could I have imagined the priceless plans that Abba had in store for me, which so often included Tom and the Hayes family. Truly, Abba is the ultimate travel companion, whose ways and purposes are unfathomable!

When Tom and I left home, we knew that we were to be devoted to prayer, watchful, and thankful. We knew that we were to proclaim Yeshua clearly and boldly and to make the most of every opportunity.

We knew that our conversation was always to be full of grace, seasoned with salt, so that we would know how to answer everyone. Colossians 4:2–6 was to be our guide. As we journeyed through the days, two figures emerged in my mind: Nehemiah and a fisherman with his net spread across his lap.

For almost thirty years, Nehemiah has been a hero of the faith to me. My first encounter with him came when I asked Abba to show me how to build a community that would be dedicated to caring for widows and orphans, a dream he had planted in my heart.

Nehemiah was the perfect example of a community builder. He saw a need, knew how to meet it, and sought God. He knew that he could not complete his task without God and others who would apply their time and talents to the project.

Today I saw an African proverb on the walls of the O. R. Tambo Airport, which I loved. It said, "If you want to go fast, go alone. If you want to go far, go together."

Nehemiah chose the latter. Interestingly, in choosing to go with others, he also went fast, miraculously rebuilding Yerushalayim's walls in only fifty-two days.

The second figure, the fisherman and his net, was similar yet different. Both individuals were builders, but Nehemiah was a community builder of physical walls, while the fisherman built a "network" of people, a community without walls.

Nehemiah was to rebuild the broken walls of Yerushalayim. The fisherman was carefully constructing his net. Some of the strands were actually broken. Some were tired and worn out from use, and some strands were brand new. The fisherman and Nehemiah lovingly, diligently built the net and the wall.

As I began to see these figures more clearly and understand their roles, something else began to dawn on me: these were pictures of Tom and me and our roles in the place where we were. This gave me great excitement, peace, and joy.

Seen through the lenses of Nehemiah and the fisherman, our daily activities took on greater substance and meaning. We were to be community builders—building a community with walls at Emmanuel Khayalethu, and developing a community *without* walls by getting to know the precious people Abba brought across our paths.

Truly the people are Abba's greatest gift to me. Each person is uniquely designed in the Father's image, each with his purpose and plan woven into his or her DNA. They are priceless treasures.

One of Nehemiah's precious qualities was a sense of celebration. When his project was completed, he called for a celebration—feasting, giving thanks, and sharing goods with each other. One day, close to the end of our stay, I was reading about the celebration. A young lady stopped by, and we chatted for a bit. Early in our visit she had asked me if I would come to bless the house that she and her husband were building. I was honored!

As we talked, though, I realized how little time I had left. When I told her that we'd probably have to postpone the blessing until our next visit, her reply totally convicted me. She said, "But Madam, you promised." It was said with love, and it went straight to my heart! We quickly chose a date—Resurrection Day/Feast of First Fruits—and we devised a plan. We would bless the house and then have cake and juice. She would invite family and friends. Just thinking about it makes me cry tears of joy to have had such a privilege. The afternoon was beautiful, and I had the priceless opportunity to bless our friends and their new house, which is still being built.

I love taking Abba at his word and then watching him bring it into existence. God promised Noah a rainbow as a sign of his covenant. God said, "This is the sign of the covenant I have established between me and all life on earth."

One day Tom and I were driving along a major highway, and Abba gave us the right half of a beautiful rainbow. On another day, my girlfriend Celeste and I were walking out of EMK when Anthony came running to show us a beautiful rainbow. This time it was the *left* side!

Remembering our first rainbow half, I was in awe of our heavenly Father. After all, who but he could put together one rainbow over the course of a number of days. It was such a beautiful expression and reminder of God's love and faithfulness.

Many years ago God gave me a promise that I would be his witness in Yerushalayim, Judea, Samaria, and to the ends of the earth. For me the rainbow was the sign of his promise, which I have experienced in Yerushalayim, throughout Israel, and most recently in Swaziland.

Please join me in praising and thanking him for all he is and for all he does.

From the ends of the earth,

Priscilla

63

"Oh, No, Not Cancer Again!"

April 22, 2013

Hello, Magnificent One,

"Hi."
"Hi."
"How are you?"
"Fine."

This could be an English 101 lesson, or it could be an everyday conversation. Lately, when people ask Tom how he is, he says, "Fine." After all, he looks fine, feels fine, has no pain, has a great appetite, can work rings around men half his age, and sleeps well! Oh, and he can still hit a golf ball a mile. So, what's the problem? He's *not* fine.

Via a bone scan, which Tom had last Monday, we have learned that our old enemy, prostate cancer, has reared its ugly head once again.

What to do this time? First, there is a new medicine in pill form called abiraterone acetate, more commonly known as Zytiga which he plans to take. Second, we plan to go on *The Maker's Diet*, a wonderful way to eat/live at any time. And third, we plan to keep our eyes on Yeshua and see how he shows us to go. Not necessarily in that order!

The Word of God has been a comfort and source of strength to us for a long time, and we are confident that it will continue to be so.

When we were in Swaziland, I visited a couple of schools that are under the direction of a new acquaintance. In each class, she had the children say their "confessions" for me. At first I thought it strange, but when I realized what their confessions were, I understood and realized the great value. They were declaring truth from Scripture, not itemizing their sins.

These "confessions" would strengthen them, help them to see how God sees them, and fill their minds with those things that are true, noble, and right. We will do the same. These verses, all taken from the Complete Jewish Bible (CJB), immediately came to mind, and they will be our daily declarations:

1. A tranquil mind gives life to the body (Proverbs 14:30).

2. A cheerful glance brings joy to the heart, and good news invigorates the bones (Proverbs 15:30).

3. A happy heart is good medicine, but low spirits sap one's strength (Proverbs 17:22).

4. "I have said these things to you so that, united with Me, you may have shalom. In the world you will have tsuris [trouble]. But be brave! I have overcome the world" (John 16:33).

5. "They defeated him because of the Lamb's blood and because of the message of their witness" (Revelation 12:11a).

Although we are disappointed with the news of the cancer itself, we are glad to know the truth of Tom's health. It is always better to know the truth, even when we don't like it, than to live in deception, because armed with the truth we can do what needs to be done. Knowing the one who is the truth, we can have confidence to face whatever happens next.

We wanted you to hear this news from us, and now you know what we know. If you think of us, please pray that we will be faithful in little things and faithful in bigger things. In all and through all, we know that our God is a good God, and we know that he is good all the time. We also know that nothing can separate us from his love.

We are grateful for you and your presence in our lives.

Here comes a hug …

Tom and *Priscilla*

64

Deliverance

that deliverance comes by having sins forgiven
through our God's most tender mercy.
—Luke 1:77b–78a

May 12, 2013

Dear Magnificent One,

It is a beautiful day here at The Homestead. I have been here the last few days so I could put this book together. What a beautiful time it has been. I am truly grateful for the generosity of our great Abba and my precious husband.

Last night I experienced the above scripture in a most embarrassing and humbling but beautiful way. Driving home from dinner, I looked into my rearview mirror to see a police car with flashing lights following me. I hate that sight, because it scares me and makes me anxious.

I assumed that he was on his way to a fire or some other noble venture. Wrong! When I finally found a place to pull off the road, he pulled in behind me. He was after *me*!

When he got out of his car, I got even more afraid, because he was a giant of a man, loaded with his police paraphernalia. My heart sank at the sight.

I was amazed when the first words out of his mouth were, "You probably have no idea why I pulled you over, do you?" Right on. I was clueless. It was a beautiful night, I'd had a lovely time at dinner, and the music on my CD player soothed my soul. All was right in my world. What possible reason could he have to stop me? He took my license and registration and went back to his car.

When he returned, he bent down to talk with me. Somehow he wasn't so scary anymore. Then he totally surprised me. He told me that he would just give me a warning this time. I was so relieved, because I knew he could have given me a hefty fine.

Mercy and grace poured out of this officer as he repeatedly said, "Please slow down. I don't want you to get hurt." When I thanked him for doing his job, he simply said that he wanted to protect me and the others on the road. I was so grateful, and I wanted him to know that.

What he didn't know was that I saw Abba's tender mercy and forgiveness in him. Because of his tender mercy, I was forgiven of my sin and delivered of my fear and anxiety.

Sadly, I don't know the officer's name, but I will always remember his grace, gentle mercy, and forgiveness. Even as he walked away, he encouraged me to drive slowly. I promised him I would.

You know, dear Magnificent One, this officer so reminded me of Abba. Abba corrects us, protects us, warns us, encourages us, and pours his grace upon us. And you know what? It makes me love him all the more.

Thank you for traveling this journey to Abba's heart with me. I am grateful for your companionship.

Gratefully,

Priscilla

PS: Timeliness is such an important part of life. One thing I have learned about God is that he is always on time—never late, never early, but always *on time.* You can see, dear one, that although my desire was to publish this book in 2013, it seems I had to learn to persevere until the *fullness of time*, the *right* time.

I am reminded of my African friend who told me that in the West we have watches, but in Africa they have time! May we always have time for God and for his plans. We will be amazed!

65

Keeping Cool

July 17, 2013

Providence Farm

> The fig trees are forming their unripe figs,
> and the grapevines in bloom give out their perfume.
> Get up, my love, my beauty! Come away!"
> —Song of Solomon 2:13

Dear Magnificent Sevens,

I hope this finds you well and keeping cool in the warmth of Abba's love. I hope too that the time you were able to have with Abba on the seventh was a blessing to you. I know that Abba is blessed when we make these special appointments with him. Isn't it wonderful to know that Almighty God, the creator of all that exists, wants to have special appointments with us? I find that truly amazing.

I would love to hear how Abba spoke to you, if you would like to say. And I would like to tell you what happened here. If you have a moment, here goes:

As it was a Sunday, I had the dilemma of deciding whether to go to church or stay home. I decided to stay home, and I'm glad I did. Having that time alone with Abba was a delight.

Here are the highlights of the day:

1. Thanksgiving time brought Psalm 67 to mind. It is reminiscent of Numbers 6:24–26, which is a blessing for Israel. We are clearly told in scripture that through Israel all nations of the world will be blessed. The greatest blessing of all is our beloved Savior, Yeshua, reconciling us to the Father and giving us the Holy Spirit to be with us forever! Thanks be to God!

2. During our time of confession, the Ten Commandments kept coming to mind. Not that they came in order, but as we confessed the sins of the nation, I realized that all ten have been clearly broken. In addition, we have committed the sins of arrogance and pride, a critical spirit, and being judgmental. Truly we are a nation in need of a Savior.

   Fortunately, we have a Savior who cleanses us from all sin and makes us righteous in the sight of almighty God, our beloved Father. A freshly washed pile of sheets reminded me of how good cleanliness feels and how effective it is.

3. Praying for Israel brought to mind her leaders: the prime minister, the president, mayors of Yerushalayim, Bethlehem, Jericho, Tel Aviv, and Arad. We must also pray for the leaders of the nations that are openly committed to her destruction.

4. Praying for the families of believers brought to mind the many leaders who have been part of my spiritual journey. God was gracious to give me many wonderful ones.

In closing I would like to leave you with a part of the prayer of Yeshua in John 17: 20–21: "I pray not only for these, but also for those who will trust in me because of their word, that they may all be one. Just as you, Father, are united with me, and I with you, I pray that they may be united with us, so that the world may believe that you sent me."

Thanks for being magnificent, dear one.

Poppa loves you! Yeshua said so, and I agree!

66

Accentuate the Positive

August 1, 2013

Dear Magnificent Sevens,

Can you believe that our day of prayer and fasting is here again on Wednesday, the seventh? Has your summer flown by? Mine has! I am excited that we will have our day once again.

At the moment, Tom and I are in Colorado, where we will have a whole week visiting friends. What joy that will be! It does, however, pose a bit of a problem: how will I be able to pray and fast with you on Wednesday?

Once again, our beloved Holy Spirit has provided a way. As fasting meals might be difficult, I can fast from *negativity*! I can fast negative thoughts, words, and actions. It is not a new idea. The first time I heard of it was years ago when one of our Magnificent Sevens told me she was doing that for the forty days of Lent. I thought then that it sounded like a great thing to do.

The idea was brought to mind again when Tom and I were in Swaziland this winter, and again recently in a letter from Bridges for Peace. It came up again yesterday in a conversation with our daughter Emily. I think the Holy Spirit just might be on to something wonderful in all of this.

When we turn the negatives to positives, we see Romans 8, which says that Abba will use for good everything that happens to his children. When we turn the negatives to positives, we see Romans 8, which says that Abba will use for good everything that happens to his children.

So, dear one, won't you join me? If you begin to have a negative thought about someone, pray for that one, even if that someone is yourself! If you start to think negatively about something, ask Abba to show you how to convert the negative into a positive. One thing I know: you will feel better than you will if the negativity takes charge.

Last month we *talked* about praying for our enemies. Let's be doing that as the Holy Spirit shows us *who* they are and *how* to pray for them. Again, we will turn negatives to positives!

It's good to be doing this together. Thanks for joining me.

May you richly enjoy all the blessings that Abba has in store for you today, on Wednesday, and every day.

Grateful for you,

Priscilla

67

Every Second Counts

October 6, 2013

Dear Magnificent Sevens,

Wow! It's that time of the month again: Monday, the seventh, our seven-to-seven day of prayer and fasting, and I am so excited to write to you.

Last Sunday Tom and I and seven of our fellow travelers returned to the USA from Israel, where I had the glorious experience of turning seventy years old! I can't remember being so excited about a birthday. Age seventy is a huge milestone. Thanks be to God for the milestone—and that it happened in Yerushalayim! God has given us seventy years, and any additional years are icing on the cake.

As I thought about being seventy, I thought, *there are ten sevens in seventy; there are seven tens in seventy, and there is one seventy.* So what?

Numbers in scripture are important and have meaning and pattern, both of which help us to understand how amazing God is. He is *awesome.* No one else and nothing else is worthy of the description *awesome.*

I am a novice in this area and am excited to learn more about the whole subject of biblical numbers.

I also figured that there are 2,207,520,000 seconds in seventy years! Again you might ask, "So what?"

To that question, I would answer this: God knows every one of those seconds! He knows every minute, every hour, every day, and every year of my existence and yours. That shouts of an infinitesimally involved God. It shouts to me of a loving heavenly Father who watches over every moment of every day of our lives. It shouts to me that I am not nothing in God's sight—and neither are you.

It shouts to me, "I care."

Love so amazing, so divine, demands and deserves everything from me: my time, my energy, my devotion, and my love. I want to give him my all. How about you?

As we pray for Israel, let's keep these precious people in mind: Israel's leaders in government, in families, and in every segment of society, and our precious friends who are actually *family* to us.

As we pray for Providence Farm, please pray for the Women of Prayer Weekend, which we will host October 18 to 20. I am very excited about this weekend. The theme is "I Will Follow," and we will follow the book of Ruth. Please remember all of our guests, the speakers, and our chefettes—and the myriad of details that must be attended to.

You really are magnificent, you know, and I am eternally grateful for you! I don't know how many seconds there are in eternity, but this I know: our loving heavenly Father will be with us every second of it. Now that's something to shout and sing about.

Love and hugs are flying your way,

68

Prayer Changes Us

November 2, 2013

Dear Magnificent One,

It's a beautiful day in the neighborhood of Providence Farm. It's Shabbat, and there is a godly peace that surrounds me as I write to you. The leaves are wearing their beautiful autumn coats of many colors, the air is clear and brisk, and the mountains are standing in their glory. Ah, yes, God is good.

However, I am painfully aware that all is not bright and beautiful in all of God's world. As Tom and I discussed his health situation and how he is affected by the medical community, I am reminded that many in our midst are experiencing great trials concerning their health. We are having our own challenge once again as we have recently learned that although Tom "feels fine," tests show that he is *not* fine. In fact, the tests show that once again cancer has invaded his body in his lymph nodes and in his bones. The doctor has prescribed new medication and says that Tom has an 80 percent chance of the cancer going into "durable remission." Pretty good odds, I'd say.

Tom's medication is pricey, and I am grateful that we have a heavenly Father who knows our needs and provides for them. We recently leased space to a new tenant, and an old tenant is stepping up and paying back rent. These are very practical answers to our prayers. Praise God from whom all blessings flow.

Last month's Women of Prayer Weekend was a time to experience God's grace, beauty, and presence. I really cannot speak for any of the other ladies, but this I know: Abba blessed me beyond my wildest imaginings. The camaraderie among the ladies was precious to see. The teachings enlightened and inspired me—definitely delicious food for the soul. And the chefettes fed our bodies with delicious and nutritious goodies. The times of prayer, both corporate and individual, were precious, and I know that Abba was listening and that he will respond.

After the prayer weekend, Tom and I motored to Savannah, Georgia, where Tom played in a senior amateur golf tournament, and we had the joy of reconnecting with old friends and making new ones. It was a beautiful time of resting and regrouping, and that is always good.

As we drove, we read a book called "Red Moon Rising" which had been recommended by Magnificent Seven Liz. It's about twenty-four seven prayer, and a movement that has recently been catching fire around the globe.

Incessant prayer is not a new concept. The disciples prayed and praised God for days in the temple after the ascension of Yeshua. Anna, the widow, "worshipped, prayed and fasted night and day, never leaving the Temple grounds" (Luke 2:36). The Moravians in Germany started a twenty-four seven prayer meeting that lasted more than one hundred years. In each of these instances, people were gathered together in one place.

Last month, other Magnificent Sevens joined me in the chapel. There is power in prayer, and there is power in being together in one place. Therefore, I am inviting you to join me in the chapel on Thursday, November 7, for our time of prayer and fasting. Please come for all or any part of the day. I would especially invite you to come for the six p.m. to seven p.m. time of celebration. I realize that we will not all be able to gather here at the farm, because we live in many areas of the globe, but for those who are near, please come by.

In 2 Chronicles, chapter 7, God appeared to Solomon and promised him: "Then, if my people, who bear my name, will humble themselves, pray, seek my face and turn from their evil ways, I will hear from heaven, forgive their sin, and heal their land" (2 Chronicles 7:14).

As those who "bear his name," may we gather together to humble ourselves, seek his face, repent for ourselves and our nations, and pray. And may he hear our prayers and heal our lands.

Once again, leaning on the direction of the Holy Spirit, we will follow the schedule of ACTS:

Adoration: 7:00–8:00 a.m.
Confession: 8:00–9:00 a.m.
Thanksgiving: 9:00–10:00 a.m.
Supplication: 10:00 a.m.–6:00 p.m.

We will pray together according to this schedule:

10:00–11:00 a.m.: Israel
11:00 a.m.–12:00 p.m.: our own needs
Noon–1:00 a.m.: our families
1:00–2:00 p.m.: our own nation
2:00–3:00 p.m.: Yeshua's disciples throughout the world—especially those who are persecuted for their faith—and for unity among us
3:00–4:00 p.m.: our enemies
4:00–5:00 p.m.: widows and orphans
5:00–6:00 p.m.: world leaders
6:00–7:00 p.m.: Praise, thanksgiving, and communion

You are magnificent, dear one, and I thank
God for the gift that you are.

Priscilla

69

Wonder of Wonders

January 17, 2014

Dear Magnificent One,

Wonder of wonders, a real *wow*: that was what our day of prayer and fasting was for me, and I hope it was for you as well. I came away from the day, shaking my head at the way the Holy Spirit orchestrated our time, knowing that he had done it, because there was no other way the day could have transpired the way it did.

The day started with reading Revelation 4, the wonderful throne room scene where the elders and the living beings are singing God's praises. I love the part that describes the four living beings: one was like a lion, one was like an ox, the third had a face that looked human, and the fourth was like a flying eagle. No sooner had I finished reading this than our wonderful golden retriever dog, Rachy (Rachmaninov), wanted to come into the chapel and keep me company. Ah, yes, even the four-footed beings can praise him!

Praying for "the peace of Yerushalayim" during our time of prayer for Israel took me to a phone conversation with our brother and friend Todd, who lives in Israel. After our conversation I had a great peace concerning the timing of our trip with two of our granddaughters to

Israel. I realized that indeed "the peace of Yerushalayim"—the Prince of Peace, Yeshua—had given me peace concerning our travel dates. He is faithful.

During our time to pray for the church, we were led to pray for healing in the church. Many people in the family of God personally need healing of spirit, soul, or body. In the midst of praying, Tom came home from his doctor's appointment. He has a new oncologist, whom he started seeing last fall. His report was glorious. For the first time since 2005 when we first learned that cancer had attacked Tom, the doctor said, "When we kill this thing, we are going to do this …" His conclusion was that *Tom could be healed*!

Now, even though the first doctor had told Tom that the cancer was incurable, we have always known that God could heal him completely! We later learned that his PSA, which is the big marker for his type of cancer, had been significantly reduced, going from a high of 9 to the low of 0.8. The biblical number eight has the significance of "new life" or "resurrection." Our faith level was increased exponentially. And our gratitude level escalated as well. Truly, God is good.

It is my prayer that as you participate in these Magnificent Sevens days you will experience the loving presence of our priceless Savior; that you will know the height, the depth, the breadth, and the length of his love for you. Our prayers may not be noted by many, but they're noted by the One and Only, and he delights to spend time communing with us. Isn't that just the most wonderful news? Yes!

You are *magnificent*!

Priscilla

70

Highlights of the Day

To God be the glory, great things he has done!

April 9, 2014

Dear Magnificent One,

Grace and peace to you from God our Father, our Savior Yeshua, and the Holy Spirit who lives with us.

I trust that you had a blessed day on Monday, wherever you were. It was a great blessing for me, as Tom and I spent the day in the chapel, joined at different points by our "magnificent ones" Jennifer and Doc. Whenever I think about it, I am overwhelmed by the fact that God invites us to meet with him and that he shares what is on his heart and mind with us so we can talk with him (pray) about it.

If you have a moment, I would like to share some of the high points with you.

1. Confession began with this commandment: "Do not give false evidence against your neighbor," which boiled down to "Do not lie." Tom and I had just heard a sermon on Sunday about this commandment. It made me wonder: how do I lie? Do I

exaggerate? Do I leave out details or add them in? What lies have I believed about God, myself, or others? Whether telling a lie, or believing and acting on one, lying is wrong. It needs to be confessed, forgiven, and stopped. Confession is a great gift from the Father, as it affords us the way to forgiveness and restoration of our relationship with him.

2. The second highlight for me came in the afternoon as we prayed for the persecuted church. Tom and I realized how little we know about this topic, so I decided to Google it. It was amazing how God used the Internet as we prayed during the day. We were led to a website where they have a prayer map. Because of relationships we have in Belarus and Uganda, we decided to see what was going on there.

Sad to say, we found reason to pray for the precious brothers and sisters in these two countries. When we clicked on "Uganda" and then on "Pastor Update," we were surprised to see an article about a pastor we had seen in Israel in 2012. He had attended the Feast of Tabernacles celebration hosted by the International Christian Embassy Yerushalayim, where we first heard his story. Muslims had thrown acid on his face and his back. His is a heartrending story, but one of the beautiful sides is the gracious medical help he has been given in Israel.

3. Being led by the Holy Spirit was the greatest joy of all. Although we came with the agenda of ACTS, we didn't know how to pray specifically in each area. We needed the Holy Spirit to show us, and he did. Sometimes he used scripture, sometimes he led us to use the Internet, and sometimes he inspired a thought about someplace or someone.

It was my hope and prayer that as we prayed—whether here on the farm or wherever you were—that we would each draw closer to the Father, hear his voice, and respond to him. We hoped that as we did so, we would all grow in wisdom, knowledge, and love of him. I hope you did. I know I did.

Thank you for taking the time to share these thoughts so that we might rejoice together in God's great goodness. To him be the thanks, the honor, the power, and the praise.

You are priceless, Magnificent One!

Love and hugs for the journey,

71

The Gift of Tears

August 3, 2014

Psalm 34

Dear Magnificent One,

Grace and peace to you from God our Father and our Lord Yeshua, the Messiah.

Sending you warm greetings from our beautiful Providence Farm. We have had a wonder-filled summer. We took our two eldest grands, Lexy and Megan, to Israel. We hosted a precious Young Life family for a month while they took necessary steps to be able to return to the work that Abba has for them in Scotland. We held our last Magnificent Sevens day in July, and I heard the ringing of my *Red Alert: Israel* app reminding me to pray for Israel.

Our last Magnificent Sevens day found me in tears for a good part of the day, a gift from our Abba. Some were tears of joy as sisters joined me, and some were sad tears for my lack of tears over sin in my own life and in the world. I realized that my normal reaction to sin is anger, which doesn't always accomplish God's purposes. Unlike the experiences of Nehemiah, Joel, and Yeshua himself, sin rarely, if ever, prompted *me* to tears. But bless God that on July 7, by his grace, I did experience those tears. It was a wonderful day, and I praise God for the gift that it was. He certainly made his presence known as he guided the day. To him be glory, honor, and praise.

So please join me this Thursday, August 7, at 7:00 a.m. to 7:00 p.m. I will be at the chapel on our Providence Farm. Join me there if you can, or please be in prayer where you are.

The following is our proposed agenda so that we might be praying in concert with each other, wherever we are.

7:00 a.m. - Putting on the whole armor of God (Ephesians 6:10–20), righteousness and faithfulness (Isaiah 11:5), and righteousness, salvation, vengeance, and zeal (Isaiah 59:17)
8:00 a.m. - *Adoration* (Psalm 34)
9:00 a.m. - *Confession* (Psalm 51)
10:00 a.m. - *Thanksgiving* (Psalm 100)
11:00 a.m.–6:00 p.m. - *Supplication/intercession* (1 Timothy 2:1–5; Psalm 72; Psalm 122; Matthew 5:11–12, 43–48)
11:00 a.m. - Israel (Psalm 91)
Noon - World leaders
1:00 p.m. - Ourselves
2:00 p.m. - Families
3:00 p.m. - The family of God, and especially those who are being tortured and put to death for their faith
4:00 p.m. - Providence Farm
5:00 p.m. - Widows and orphans
6:00 p.m. - Praise and communion

You have a high calling, precious one, to come boldly to the throne of grace to seek God for yourself, your family, your city, state, nation, and world. It is God who calls you to his glorious self. Be blessed in him.

Grace and peace to you for the journey,

72

The Beauty of Communion

August 8, 2014

Dear Magnificent One,

Grace and peace to you from God our Father and from our Lord, Yeshua!

When you think of prayer, do you think of it as being a monologue or a dialogue? Is it one or the other? Or can it be both? I used to think that it was a monologue where I could just pour out what was in my heart and mind to God.

Years ago, as part of a group who prayed together monthly for the nations, I learned the beauty of prayer as dialogue. I learned the joy and the reality that God really does speak if I will only listen to him and listen *for* him. Amazing! The one who created everything wants to commune with us!

Yesterday I saw the beauty and power of spending the day in communion with Abba. It was a most beautiful day as there were times when he spoke, though not audibly, to me. There were times when I spoke to him. There were times of quiet, and times of singing, dancing, and clapping. There were times with others and times of solitude. There were times of correction as Holy Spirit showed me my sin, and there were times of forgiveness and cleansing. There were times of joy and celebration. There was time simply to be in his presence.

I praise God for the gift of communion with him and with family and friends. It is priceless!

Be blessed, dear one. Your heavenly Father desires communion with you. Enjoy him.

He lives!

Priscilla

73

O LORD, God of Isra'el!

May 9, 2013

> "But you will receive power when the Ruach HaKodesh comes upon you; and you will be my witnesses both in Yerushalayim, and in all Y'hudah and Shomron, indeed to the ends of the earth."
> —Acts 1:8

Dear Magnificent One,

I can still remember the first time I went to Israel more than thirty years ago. It was life changing. I still remember saying to Abba, "Lord, one day I want to come back here and live like the people do. I don't want to be a tourist. I want to go where they go and do what they do." I have not yet lived in Israel, though I have visited on a number of occasions. Perhaps one day ...

My last trip was in September and October of 2012, when a group of us went to Yerushalayim to celebrate the Feast of Tabernacles, known in Hebrew as *Sukkot*. Once again, it would be a trip that proved to be life changing.

What made these trips life changing? Abba himself and his presence there. The opportunity to see scripture lived out in my own life always changes me and makes me realize how real and how present Abba is.

It was in 1977 that I had a very dramatic encounter with the Holy Spirit, which radically changed my life. God became real to me; before that, he had been a great idea. Oh, I knew he existed, but I had no idea of his relevance in my life or anyone else's. That is, until I encountered his Spirit.

Suddenly the Bible had a draw and a fascination for me that I'd never had before. The words almost leaped off the pages. I didn't always understand them, but there was something about them that soothed the soul or encouraged my faintheartedness. It was real, and it was alive, and it was for *now*.

Suddenly I had a deep desire to go to Israel, the place where Abba said he dwells. It was there that I would realize the words of Acts 1:8. I did *see* him there. I did *hear* him there. I witnessed him in very real, tangible ways.

For a long time, I had desired that Tom and I renew our wedding vows, but we had not had an opportunity to do so. While on a tour in Israel with a number of church folks, we were given the opportunity to be baptized in the Jordan River if we'd never been baptized. For those of us who had been baptized, there would be an opportunity to have blessings spoken over us. I liked that.

When it came time for the blessings, we were asked to divide up into three groups so that each priest would have a group to pray over, thus simplifying and expediting the process.

I got in one line, and Tom got in another. He is so adorable, not moved by *fame*. As I stood in line, a quiet thought entered my mind, but I knew that it was Abba speaking. "Get in line with Tom," said the voice.

"I don't want to," was my reply. Can you imagine that, arguing with the Most High God? Well, I did it—not once, not twice, but *three* times. Oh, how patient is our Abba.

Grudgingly, I agreed to respond to the voice. I moved into line with Tom. We inched closer to our *blessing*, and finally it was our turn. Gently the priest put his arms around our shoulders and drew us closer to each other. Then, the most astounding words came out of his mouth: "And those whom God has joined together, let no man put asunder."

Tom and I looked at each other, and Tom said, "Well, I guess we don't have to do that again, do we?"

Why did the priest do that? How did he know that such a desire was in my heart? I didn't even know the man. Later at dinner, I had a chance to ask him about what had happened. When I asked him why he'd done what he did, he replied that he just thought Abba wanted him to. Simple.

There are so many other wonderful stories to tell of Abba's goodness on that trip and others that I have taken to Israel, but time and space do not permit. But I can tell you this, dear heart: those stories only serve to help me to know the deep love that Abba has for all of us.

I have experienced and witnessed the faithfulness of the Lord, *ADONAI*, the God of Israel, the God of Avraham, Yitz'chak, and Ya'akov, and my God. I have witnessed the greatness and goodness of our Abba, beginning in Yerushalayim, Y'hudah, and Shomron—and even to the ends of the earth. All I can do is thank him. All I can do is praise him. All I can do is share his love with others. All I can do is *love* him.

Thanks to you and all our praying family and friends, partners in bringing those we love before the throne of God's amazing grace. We have asked for his grace, his provision, his healing, his peace, his joy, and yes, even his correction when needed. And thank you for sharing the times of celebration, praise, and thanksgiving. With you and through you, I have been able to draw closer to the Father's heart.

From the Father's heart and mine,

74

Sounds of Joy

January 5, 2015

Dear Magnificent One,

Grace and peace to you from God our Father and our beloved Savior. May your 2015 overflow with love, joy, and peace, which can only come from God. Blessed be his name.

What do the words *chuckle, burst out laughing, chortle, crack up, giggle,* and *guffaw* have in common? Pretty obvious, I know. They are all sounds of joy. They are all joyful noises. Did you ever think about the fact that when we make those noises we can be blessing God? We know how good we can feel when we laugh out loud with a hearty belly laugh, or even just a quiet chuckle. It brightens our face, lightens our mood, and changes an atmosphere.

Psalm 98:4 and Psalm 100:1 tell us to shout for joy, sing jubilantly, sing praises, and enter his presence with praises. Wow! Make sounds of joy *out loud.*

Just think, precious one: our joyful noises can bless the Father. They can exalt him. They can give him praise. And isn't that what we are all about? He is God, after all, which is reason number one to make a joyful noise! It delights him, which is reason number two to make a joyful noise. His Word says we should—with no explanations needed, actually—and that is reason number three. I'm sure that if we thought about it we could think of a lot more reasons to make a joyful noise to the Lord.

It is my hope and prayer for us, the Magnificent Sevens, that we will make joyful noises throughout 2015, delight our beloved Father, and in the process be blessed ourselves.

You really are priceless, you know. Hahahahahaha!

This Wednesday, January 7, we will have our first Magnificent Sevens day of 2015. Be blessed in the day, wherever you are. I will be in the chapel from 1:00 p.m. to 7:00 p.m., and you are most welcome to join me if you can.

We will continue our schedule of ACTS: adoration, confession, thanksgiving, and supplication.

As we intercede, let us first remember to pray for the peace of Yerushalayim, that the Prince of Peace will make himself real to people throughout the nation, and that his presence and power would be experienced. Let's pray for unity and harmony among the people.

Pray for leaders everywhere that they would be led by the King of Kings, that they would lead their people with righteousness, truth, and grace, and that they would have the people's best interests at heart.

Pray for our families and families throughout the world.

Pray for ourselves, that we would have a heart to love and serve the Lord with his grace, wisdom, and power.

Pray for the community of faith, that all competition and striving would cease. Pray that God will remove anti-Semitism from the church.

As always, our desire is to listen in order to learn how the Holy Spirit will lead us to pray, *that the kingdom of God will come to earth as it is in heaven.*

Thank you for your partnership in prayer that moves mountains. Last month we saw Abba break through many roadblocks.

You are priceless.

75

Ears to Hear

July 14, 2015

Dear Magnificent One,

It is a good and joyful thing to give thanks to God at any time, in any place, and for any reason. This is a time to give thanks for our last Magnificent Sevens Day on July 7. If you have a moment or two, I would like to share some of God's goodness.

It was a beautiful day, and at times we could hear the rustling of the Holy Spirit as his sweet wind rustled the trees, a gentle reminder of his presence. I was particularly reminded of this as we prayed for Providence Farm, and I was reminded of the fact that as he broods over a place, person, or group, he births new ideas among them.

The day began, of course, with our suiting up in heavenly armor, our spiritual covering. Reading through our Ephesians passage, I was impressed by the reality that it is God who is every piece of armor, for we are clothed in him. The "breastplate of righteousness" captured my thoughts, especially because the breastplate of ancient armor covered and protected the soldier's vital organs. We need God's protection today, as the enemy of our souls attacks us with arrows aimed at our hearts and the seat of our emotions, the gut.

In praying for the worldwide family of God, we read and prayed through Revelation 2 and 3, the seven letters to the seven churches. What was most important to me was this sentence: "Those who have ears, let them hear what the Spirit is saying to the Messianic Communities." This thought was repeated at the end of each letter, and it was for all of the communities. Do the letters apply to me or us?

Yeshua said the same thing while he was here on earth. "If you have ears, then hear!" (Matthew 11:15). "Those who have ears, let them hear!" (Matthew 13:9).

Some want to hear and will take time to listen. Others don't want to hear and won't take time to listen. Will I be willing to listen, however Abba chooses to speak? Or will I try to box him in and say that he can only speak in one way? Will I choose to make him and his Word the authority and standard by which I will judge what I am hearing? Listening involves actions: taking in information through the ears and then acting on what I hear. Am I willing to do both?

The day closed with the celebration of the Lord's Supper. It is a priceless reality that our salvation was *not* free, as Yeshua said that his body would be broken and his blood would be poured out—priceless, extravagant love poured out for all of creation. In celebrating his last supper, we are reminded of these great and wonderful truths.

Always remember, precious one, that you are dearly loved. Abba said so in his Word; he whispers it on the breeze; and he shows it in his acts of loving kindness and in his patience with us. Be blessed!

Grateful for you,

Priscilla

76

Conquering Overcomer

July 31, 2015

Greetings, Magnificent Sevens,

Summer is heating up, and so are events around the world. It is a time to draw near to the throne of grace, because we are in a time of great need. As enemy forces seek to thwart the plans and purposes of Almighty God, I am wonderfully reminded that he is the *sovereign ruler* over all and that through his Son we are more than conquerors. So, dear one, what do you hope to conquer? What areas do you want to be victorious in? Always remember our conquering hero and lean wholly on him, for he cares for you.

Please join me for our next Magnificent Sevens day of prayer and fasting on Friday, August 7, 2015, from 7:00 a.m. to 7:00 p.m. I will be at the chapel on our Providence Farm. Join me there if you can, or please be in prayer where you are, as you can.

Our proposed agenda for the day will be our usual: adoration, confession, thanksgiving, supplication, praise, and communion.

Prayer for the USA

> Oh, merciful Lord, forgive us and cleanse us of our prideful, arrogant ways. We have sinned against you and you only. Have mercy on us and cleanse us. Do not treat us as our great sin deserves.
>
> We are vulnerable people who sometimes neglect the most vulnerable. We are broken people who don't always pay attention to the world's brokenness. Heal us, O God, to make us better healers. Mend our rifts that we might be better builders. Cleanse our hearts so that we can clean out the damage of hurt and oppression.
>
> We are yours, O God. Help us to know this better and to live it. Thank you.

You have a high calling, magnificent one, to come boldly to the throne of grace to seek God for yourself, your family, your city, state, nation, and world. It is God who calls you to his glorious self. Be blessed in him.

In conclusion, let us focus our minds on what is good and pure, righteous and noble; and let us rejoice always, giving thanks in all circumstances, for this blesses Abba's heart.

Grace and peace to you for the journey,

77

Sound the Trumpet!

August 10, 2015

Dear Magnificent One,

Thank you for your partnership in prayer, the work that only the Father sees, which delights his heart.

This past Friday, our Magnificent Sevens day was an amazing one. The Holy Spirit led all the way, sometimes in ways that amazed or surprised me, but in all I knew that it was Holy Spirit leading, because I could never have dreamed up or planned what happened.

It was a rainy day for the most part, but the rain did not dampen my spirits. Rather, it reminded me of Abba's Word that the snow and rain fall from heaven, water the earth, and do not return void. They accomplish the purposes for which Abba sends them.

I was joined in the chapel by Tom and Doc, both Naval Academy graduates, which for me was significant, as there was definitely a *military* message in the day. During our *suiting up in heavenly armor* hour, Abba gave me a picture in my mind of an army gathered and being reviewed by the commander in chief (CIC). The army was faceless, vast, uncountable. The CIC was not visible, but I could feel him. He was reviewing his troops, looking for the tired, the wounded, the broken, the strong and healthy, and those ready for battle. He was great and powerful yet compassionate and considerate of his troops. Abba, *Adonai*, the Lord of heaven's armies is, of course, the CIC, and committed believers in Yeshua are the army.

Then God showed me the divisions in the army:

1. Worshippers: singers, dancers, praisers
2. Pray-ers: the soldiers who fight the battles "on their knees" in the throne room of the Almighty
3. Emissaries: those faithful believers who go into the marketplaces (the world) and bring the Good News of the gospel
4. Medical Corps: the army's healers
5. Intelligence Corps: those who gather the information that the pray-ers need to pray intelligently with the Word of God.

God said that our weapons are not carnal but are powerful for tearing down strongholds. They consist of singing, praising, thanksgiving, and the Word of God—the Son of God and his written Word.

Our armor is *Yeshua*. He is our salvation, our helmet. He is our righteousness, our breastplate. He is the truth, our belt. He is our peace, our shoes. He is our faith, the shield with which we can deflect any fiery darts. He is the Word of God, the sword of the Spirit, and our only offensive weapon.

God showed me battlefronts in the USA: abortion, racism, and anti-Semitism in the church. The root of all problems in the USA is rebellion against God himself. Many of us in the USA have lost or detached ourselves from—or have never had—God as our spiritual compass. We need to turn to him.

The battle that rages daily is between God and his enemy, the devil. We fight alongside our CIC, and we get caught sometimes in the crossfire. Yeshua, the Good Shepherd, gives us abundant life, even as the enemy comes to kill, steal, and destroy.

During the time to pray for ourselves, I fell sound asleep on the chapel floor! *Rest* was my word for the day, and our CIC gave me his permission and the charge to rest! Prayer is work. It is warfare. And sometimes we get tired and need to sleep. When I woke up, I was ready to continue in the battle.

Abba spoke to me about abortion. He showed me a chart of the numbers of people who are involved in each abortion that is performed. Most directly involved are the baby, the mother, and the abortionist. Indirectly involved are the father, nurse/staff of the abortionist, grandmother(s), grandfather(s), siblings, extended family, and friends. Multiplied by the number of abortions performed each day, the number of people involved directly or indirectly in each abortion is staggering. These folks are all in need of grief counseling for their loss. Some need to repent and know God's forgiveness and mercy, which only he can grant. This battlefront knows no boundaries, and it is even found in the church.

Many years ago, the director of a pregnancy center in Washington, DC, told me, "For a woman who has had an abortion, the church is a dangerous and fearful place. She fears judgment, ostracism, and anger." She also told me that one in four women in the church has had an abortion or has been involved in one indirectly. I have seen those numbers borne out.

The challenge to the church is to provide a safe place for those affected by abortion to come to find God, the grace of confession and repentance, the grace of forgiveness, and the grace of freedom.

Our time of praying for Israel provided some teaching moments as well as intercession.

At one point, I was struck by that day's date: 8/7/15. Eight is the number of new beginnings, seven is the number of perfection, and fifteen is the number of rest; and of course, 8+7=15. I am experiencing new beginnings, and they are beginning with rest.

Finally, as we prayed for Providence Farm we prayed for the Women of Prayer Weekend, which we will host here August 14–16. Twenty ladies plan to gather here, with our theme being "Hear My Prayer." Please pray for safety, for travel graces, and for Abba's word to be spoken, heard, and applied. Pray for Abba to be glorified in thought, word, and deed. Pray that we will enter the throne room and dialogue with our heavenly Father. May his kingdom come. May his will be done for the glory of his name, for the maturing of his daughters, and for the expansion of his kingdom.

You have a high calling, precious one, to be with the *most magnificent one*. Draw close to him, and he will draw close to you. Be blessed, for you are precious and most dearly loved. Abba said so!

Grateful for you,

PS: I asked the ladies to pray for Providence Farm to be debt free. In December, on our Magnificent Sevens prayer day, Tom and I paid off the mortgages on the farm. Debt free at last! Oh, thank God, we are debt free at last!

You can read more about this miracle in the next letter: "It's Not About the Money."

78

It's Not About the Money

December 16, 2015

Dear Magnificent One,

This December's Magnificent Sevens day was most miraculous. It was very appropriate that it was the first day of Hanukkah, the celebration of God's miracle performed for the ancient Hebrews. Yeshua celebrated Hanukkah, so it is noteworthy for us as well.

Hanukkah celebrates the miracle God completed through a family dedicated to loving and serving him, the God of Avraham, Yitz'chak, and Ya'akov. It celebrates the miracle of God's provision of oil so that there would be light in the temple, which had been cleansed and rededicated.

So, on this first day of Hanukkah, Tom and I were given a miracle: our farm, debt free! It was an overwhelmingly wonderful feeling. Gratitude and joy flooded us. God had done what he had promised: he had given us the land as our inheritance.

Not only were we able to become completely debt free, but we had money to give away. Abba's extravagant love was not just for us.

The feeling of joy and gratitude we experienced was not about the money. It wasn't even about being debt free. It was about the God who is faithful, the God who still does miracles. It was about the God who loves graciously and extravagantly! It was about seeing God's hand in our lives.

As we approach the time to celebrate the most extravagant gift ever given, may we give him the most extravagant gift we can ever give. Let us give ourselves afresh to him. Let us rededicate ourselves to him and to his purposes.

Oh, come, let us adore him!

May you richly enjoy all the blessings our heavenly Father has in store for you today and every day. May you draw near to him, and he will draw near to you.

Love and hugs are flying your way for today and every day,

79

What Are the Chances?

January 26, 2016

Dear Magnificent One,

Please allow me to introduce myself. My name is Moshe (Moses), and I am Priscilla's new guitar! Since the day we met, we have had a great time together. I would like to tell you about how we got together. It happened this way.

For a long time, Priscilla wanted a guitar that she could travel with, one that would be small but would have a sound rich enough to praise the Lord. The last trip to Israel made her realize that a smaller guitar would be just the thing.

When she and Tom arrived in California and realized that neither of them had packed her guitar, it was a no-brainer. Now was the time for a new guitar. But which guitar? There were so many to choose from, online and in the two stores here in the area. Priscilla was *confused*!

Priscilla sought advice from our friend Shahar, who wisely wrote that she should just "play one and see if the magic comes out." Good advice. However, that would only work for the ones that were in local stores. Priscilla decided to ask Abba what to do. Such a novel concept.

In the early, early morning, the thought occurred to her to Google half-size guitars, which she did. To her delight and surprise, one picture popped up with all the info about the guitar, including the store where it could be found and the map to get there. What were the chances of one guitar model, one store, and the map to the store popping up? One in a million. It was clear to my friend Priscilla that her Abba had spoken. She went and bought me and named me Moshe (Mo' shay).

Until she came along, I just lived in a box on a shelf—unnamed, unloved, and unfulfilled! Now I have a new home and someone who loves me. I am fulfilling my purpose in life: to glorify God with the sounds of music.

"What are the chances" has been Priscilla's theme song since last Christmas when she studied the prophecies about Yeshua again. *What are the chances* that one man could fulfill all the prophecies about the Messiah that Yeshua did? He didn't just fulfill one or two—or even eight or ten. No, he fulfilled many, including those about his genealogy, birthplace, time of birth, name, the unusual circumstances surrounding his birth, the reason for coming, his life's work, and the fact that great persons would adore him.

This theme song, "what are the chances," has continued to resonate with her here in California, with the result being that she is keenly aware of Abba's presence every day and his intervention in hers and Tom's lives. He is alive. He is real. He is present. He is God with us, Emmanuel.

Some folks would say that these fulfilled prophecies and the guitar showing up when she Googled it are interesting *coincidences*, but Priscilla knows that they are not coincidences. She knows that Abba intervened on her behalf so she would know *by experience* his power and presence. She *knows* that Abba intervened in the course of history and sent his one and only Son so that all humanity could be realigned with him and *know* the height, depth, length, and breadth of his love—and love him in return.

And so, magnificent one, what is Abba singing to you? What is his theme song for you this year? One, I know, is "Jesus Loves Me," and the refrain goes like this:

> Yes, Jesus loves me,
> Yes, Jesus loves me,
> Yes, Jesus loves me,
> The Bible tells me so.

His love and hugs are flying your way from Priscilla,

Moshe

80

Super Bowl 50! Choices! Choices!

February 16, 2016

Hooray, Magnificent One!

Do you remember where you were on January 15, 1967? Perhaps you had not even been born then. I clearly remember where I was and what happened on that day. One event was of monumental importance to me personally: it was the day Tom and I dedicated our firstborn, our son David, to God. It was a family occasion, a celebration.

The other event of note was this: for the first time, the AFL (American Football League) and NFL (National Football League) would play a game for the national football championship title. It would become the Super Bowl. This was not actually a world-shaking event, but it would become a national pastime of monumental proportions. By the way, the Green Bay Packers won over the Kansas City Chiefs: 35 to 10.

Fast-forward to February 7, 2016, and another Super Bowl, this one hailed as the fiftieth. It would be an extravaganza, to be sure. It was also time for another happening, our Magnificent Sevens day. Although I did not send out a schedule, perhaps you took some time to fast and pray.

A couple of weeks before the seventh, Tom and I attended a new church, where the pastor taught on the book of Revelation. He was a very dynamic teacher/preacher, and Tom and I were impressed with him. He had much good to say. He made a couple of comments that especially caught my attention. One in particular pertained to prayer and fasting. He made the comment that we probably would not want to consider doing that until after the Super Bowl. Really? Why not? Why not during the whole day?

When I realized that Super Bowl Sunday, as it has come to be known, and our Magnificent Sevens Day coincided, I wondered what Tom and I should/would do? Not being a great football fan, I knew what I wanted to do. Tom is not a super fan either, but he is more of one than I am.

We talked a lot about the pastor's sermon and the implications of his comment. Finally, Tom said, "I know where you're going." He did, but I didn't! We would choose to fast and pray. This was not a huge sacrifice, as far as I was concerned. The choice was made.

Wouldn't you know that our decision would be challenged? It was. Some friends invited us to be with them to watch the game, and another friend invited us to lunch and the game. The game was not a temptation. Even all the yummy food that would be available was not a temptation. But the opportunity to have time with friends was.

Choices. Would we choose time with friends? Or would we choose time with Yeshua? Would we be faithful to the decision we'd made, or would we change our minds?

We decided to stick with our first decision, not because we are so "spiritual" or "religious," but because it was the right thing for *us* to do, and because we wanted to do it. Yes, we wanted to be with friends, for that is important. To have our Magnificent Sevens day and Super Bowl Sunday coincide was not *convenient*, and we had to make a choice. We are both thankful for the choice we made.

Prayer and fasting are wonderful ways that we can connect with Abba. The timing may not always be *convenient*, and it may involve *sacrifice*, but in the end, it is always worth it.

There are so many ways to fast, and the following is only a short list of things we can give up:

1. *Food*. We can give up our favorite food item, or solid foods, or—like Daniel—eat a more vegetarian diet for a period of time. We can do like Yeshua did and fast from solid food for forty days, or be like Moses and go without bread or water for forty days, or be like Esther and go for three days without food and water—and do it with others.

2. *Activity*. We can give up watching TV, listening to secular music, or a favorite pastime.

3. *Negative speech*. We can refuse gossip and discouraging words.

There are many ways to pray.

- We can stand, kneel, sit, or lie prostrate on the floor.
- We can praise God for who he is.
- We can thank God for who he is and what he has done.
- We can intercede for others.
- We can pray in song, whispers, or crying out in a loud voice.
- We can raise our hands in surrender.
- We can read God's Word and speak it.
- We can persevere in prayer until we receive God's answer.

There is no set amount of time, either. That is between God and the individual.

Our world is in great turmoil, and we need a mighty movement of the Holy Spirit. It will come as we pray and fast, as we spend time with the Holy One of Israel. Yeshua encouraged his disciples with these words:

"This is the kind of spirit that can be driven out only by prayer" (Mark 9:29).

Beloved, there are situations in the world and in our lives that can only be changed by prayer and fasting.

Do not grow weary in well doing. Prayer and fasting are "well doing." Do not grow weary in seeking heaven. Abba said that those who seek him will find him. And isn't it our heart's desire to be in the presence of the one and only true and living God?

Be blessed in well doing. Abba loves you, and he will say, "Well done, good and faithful servant."

81

The Ultimate Pray-er

March 18, 2016

Dear Magnificent One,

Imagine this: You have been invited into the throne room of the ultimate king, the most important being in all of creation, in all of history. The king is sitting on a glorious throne. What will you do?

I am reminded of the beloved prophet Isaiah, who experienced the throne room of the great King, God Almighty. He recognized his position and his need, and he listened to God and responded.

Do you find it amazing, dear one, that you and I can have that same opportunity today? Do you realize that we can join with angels and the heavenly company gathered around God's throne to praise him, to thank him, to ask him to do what we cannot do for ourselves or others? We can, you know, because of Yeshua, The Ultimate pray-er. He opened the way to the Father. He is the way to the Father. His is the way to pray.

Yeshua was and is the ultimate communicator. He communicated with God and man. Through his own words, we see what is on the heart of God, what his will is.

The last night that Yeshua was with his closest associates, he prayed this way:

> I pray not only for these, but also for those who will trust in me because of their word, that they may all be one. Just as you, Father, are united with me and I with you, I pray that they may be united with us, so that the world may believe that you sent me. The glory which you have given to me, I have given to them; so that they may be one, just as we are one—I united with them and you with me, so that they may be completely one, and the world thus realize that you sent me, and that you have loved them just as you have loved me. (John 17:20-23)

With these words, Yeshua allowed his closest friends and all who would see them to know the most intimate part of himself, his greatest desires.

These words—this ultimate prayer of the Ultimate Pray-er—still echo down through the ages. They still have power to reconcile. Until Yeshua's prayer is fulfilled, we can pray with him and with all the company of heaven for its fulfillment. Won't you join us?

Thank you, dear one, for going with God and me, for travelling the road of prayer with us. It has been a pleasure having you come along.

It is my greatest hope and prayer that God's kingdom will come on earth as it is in heaven, and may it begin with you and me. Amen? Amen.

Gratefully yours,

Priscilla

82

Who is the Beggar?

January 25, 2017

Dear Magnificent One,

I walked right past him. He was sitting on the concrete sidewalk outside the gas station store. Not only did I walk past him, I turned my head so that I would not look at him, as if he would disappear if I didn't look at him. Shame on me! I felt the shame in the pit of my stomach.

Walking as quickly as I could I got into the car where Tom waited for me. "Have you got a few dollars?", he asked. I checked my wallet and, no, I didn't. "Well, okay, then, I'll just use what I have.", he said, and got out of the car. Crossing the side walk he bent down and gave the man sitting on the pavement the $20 bill in his hand. Yes, the very man I had just walked past and tried to ignore. I saw the man's face light up. Tom continued on into the store and I sat in the car overwhelmed by the grace of my beloved husband! I weep even now, thinking of it.

Suddenly, without thinking about it, I found myself getting out of the car and walking over to talk with the man. I knelt down so that I could be on his eye level, where I saw tears brimming in his eyes. We began to chat.

"Ziggy" was his name. "Born in the swamps, learned to kill in the desert.", was how he described his life. And now, here he was sitting on the concrete outside a gas station store. He was a US military man, served his country in war in the desert. Wouldn't take a thank you for his service, because, "it was my duty.", he said. And, he felt privileged to serve. We chatted for another minute or two, and then I asked him if I could give him a blessing. He agreed, and I choked out my favorite blessing, the Aaronic blessing from the Book of Numbers:

> "May *Adonai* bless you and keep you.
> May *Adonai* make his face shine on you and show you his favor.
> May *Adonai* lift up his face toward you and give you peace!"
>
> Numbers 6: 24, 25, 26

I thanked him for the privilege of our visit and for blessing me, walked back to the car and got in to wait for Tom.

I will never forget "Ziggy". I have thought of him almost every day since our meeting two weeks ago. I pray that he will KNOW the height, the depth, the breadth and the length of Abba's great love for him and that he will return love to The Father.

I think of Peter and John walking up to the Temple. They saw a man crippled from birth being carried into the Temple court. They LOOKED STRAIGHT AT HIM, (unlike me), and said that they didn't have any money but they would give him what they had. And what they had was better than silver or gold. They gave him a renewed body through the name of Yeshua the Messiah! And, he got up, walked, leaped and praised God!

By God's grace, "Ziggy" and I praised God, too. *You see, truly, I was the beggar and "Ziggy" was Yeshua, Jesus, to me!* Blessed be God! God is so good and I am so grateful for his amazing grace.

Hugs for the journey,

Priscilla

83

Marching for Mankind

Friday, January 27, 2017

Dear Magnificent One,

Tom and I have just watched the 44th annual March for Life held in Washington, DC. Yes, I, the non TV viewer, sat for 3 hours and watched as thousands: men, women, and children, old and young, gathered on The Mall in Washington, DC, to declare our solidarity for life. It was a very emotional viewing, especially as I remembered that in the march twenty years ago, I was accompanied by our daughter Emily, and our first grandchild Lexy. Lexy's name Alexandra means "defender of mankind." And that is what the march is about, the defense of mankind!

I was reminded of the women who graced our home and changed my life because God called Tom and me to "start a home for unwed mothers', not knowing anything about how to do that and certainly never dreaming that we would be called to do it in our own home. Our beloved children David, Emily and Ashley stepped up to the call too, even though they were young.

I am ever grateful to CC, the first young lady to live with us. She constantly challenged me, my obedience to God and my faith. God used her dramatically to humble me and to heal me and to show me the truths of Isaiah 58: 6-14. As we opened our home to women in crisis situations, God opened my heart to know more and more of WHO HE IS and I experienced his power and presence in my life.

It wasn't always easy having others, whether family members or strangers, live with us because our lives were exposed, warts, faults and all. Would I change the lifestyle of extending our family? Never, because it blesses God's heart.

I thank GOD for the many women who have chosen life for the child in their womb, even when it was difficult to do so. I thank GOD for those who bring his love to those who have chosen abortion so that they might know the power of his love, his grace and his forgiveness.

I thank GOD for your life, Magnificent One, and for the power of your presence in my life and in this world. As you move in your spheres of influence may you know the height, the depth, the breadth and the length of The Father's great love for you, and may you continue to shed his light and love abroad in this very needy world who so desperately needs him. AND YOU!

L'Chaim!

Hugs and love are flying your way,

Priscilla

84

Have it Your Way

You are to have no other gods before me. You are not to
bow down to them or serve them;
Exodus 20:3,4,5a

March 9, 2017

Dear Magnificent One,

Who is god to you? Who is God to you? What does God look like to you?

Many years ago I sat down to write out my list of goals for the year. Not normally being a goal setter this was new territory for me. It began to look like a list of New Year's resolutions, and most would be easily broken. I looked at the list and thought, "What's wrong with this picture?" What was wrong was easily seen: they were all totally insignificant!

I went back to the drawing board. What really mattered in life? Who or what was truly important? Who or what was worthy of being a goal? I decided to revise my Goals List and it boiled down to this:

I wanted to know the God of the Scriptures and not the god of the culture.

So, what's the difference? Major. The God of the Scriptures, Yahweh, *Adonai*, is no trifling, shifting sands, this way one minute and next minute another way puppet. Nor is he a genie in a bottle waiting for me to command him. No, he is constant, consistent, holy and the ONLY ONE. He is sovereign over all of creation. He is larger than all of life yet he is intimately involved in the smallest details of life. Especially yours and mine.

We live in a society that says "Me, me, me." "I want it my way." "I'll DO IT MY WAY." "I can do it myself." We live in a world that wants to make God out to be any way they want him, any color, any race any creed. We can make ourselves and our desires god. But GOD.

But God says, "You are to have no other gods before me. You are not to bow down to them or serve them;". God says that we are to love him above all else and then we are to love people. Bless him because he teaches us what true love looks like: the person of Yeshua.

I am still not a big goal setter. One thing I desire: to know the One and Only, true God, the God of Avraham, Yitz'chak, and Ya'akov, the God of Mattityahu, (Matthew), Mark, Luke and Yochanan, (John). I have learned: it is far better to do it his way than mine. And I have learned to say, "Father in Heaven, have it your way, not mine." How about you, dear One?

Because you are precious and dearly loved,

APPENDIX

Priscilla's Prayer Timeline

1. March 28, 1977: This was the day that prayer became important to me, because God became real, personal, important, and powerful to me.

2. 1977: Tom, David, Emily, Ashley, and I prayed for world leaders, one whose name we could not even pronounce. Years later, one of his friends, who was surprised that we had prayed for him, taught us the correct pronunciation.

3. February 2, 1978: Tom and I attended our first National Prayer Breakfast in Washington, DC.

4. 1981: After moving to Arlington, Virginia, I joined with other neighborhood moms to pray for our families. Generations of relationships developed.

5. 1982: In the Prayers for the Nations (PFTN) prayer group, I learned to listen to God so that prayer became a dialogue, not just a monologue or my laundry list of requests.

6. 1982: I learned that sometimes God reveals his answers in amazing ways. Years after praying for the Mafia in Miami at a PFTN gathering in 1982, a Parisian art dealer revealed a way that God answered those prayers.

7. 1985–86: My dear friend Jana Brodnax and I began to pray for Europe and South Africa, never dreaming what would happen to us through prayer.

8. March, 1989: This was the birth of *The Family Extended Prayer Letter and Calendar.* Each month we prayed for widows and orphans around the world, and for the groups who served them. Each month had a continental focus as well, so we prayed around the world annually.

9. April 17, 1996: I was in the parents' waiting room, praying for our first grandchild to be safely and swiftly born. She was! The birth of each grandchild was a special occasion that provided opportunity to pray and give thanks for each one.

10. January–February 2002: I learned to ask God how to pray for the prostitutes I had the privilege of praying for as we visited with them in Cape Town, South Africa.

11. January 2005: We began praying for Tom's healing from stage 4 prostate cancer.

12. April 2006: Tom and I and our prayer partners began to pray that we would have Providence Farm debt free. (On December 7, 2015, we paid off the mortgages.)

13. December 2011: I decided to start Magnificent Sevens. January 7, 2012, was our first day.

14. February 2012: I attended the first Bridges for Peace Women of Prayer Weekend.

15. August 2013, 2014, and 2015: We hosted Bridges for Peace Women of Prayer Weekends at Providence Farm.

16. October 2015: Teaching in Israel about the prayer of Daniel was a special joy. I love the prayers of Daniel, Nehemiah, Sha'ul, and

most of all, Yeshua. These biblical giants are the perfect models of prayer, and I use their prayers often, especially those of Yeshua.

17. January 2016: A small group of us began a *Harp and Bowl*, a time of prayer based on Revelation 4–5.

18. Every Day Possible: Tom and I have regular times to pray together on a daily basis. It is difficult to stay angry or separated from someone you pray with and for whom you pray. This is my great joy: having a husband who prays with me and for me and our family.

19. Every Friday Possible: We pray for the peace of Jerusalem.

20. Every Trip: Whenever Tom and I travel, we know that friends and family are praying for me/us every step of the way, from planning through completed travel. We have been privileged to pray in Argentina, Austria, Belarus, Brazil, Canada, England, France, Germany, Ireland, Israel, Kenya, Mexico, Northern Ireland, Peru, Rwanda, Scotland, South Africa, Swaziland, and Uganda. What, where and when will be next?

Glossary

Hebrew	*English*
Abba	Father
ADONAI	LORD; GOD; YAHWEH
Avraham	Abraham
Beit-Lechem	Bethlehem
Isra'el	Israel
Marta	Martha
Miryam	Mary
Natzeret	Nazareth
Ruach HaKodesh	Holy Spirit
Sha'ul	Paul
Shomron	Samaria
Y'hudah	Judea
Ya'akov	Jacob
Yerushalayim	Jerusalem
Yeshua	Jesus
Yitz'chak	Isaac
Yosef	Joseph

Final Words

May the grace of the Lord Yeshua be with you!
—Revelation 22:21

About the Author

Priscilla Flory loves to dream! She dreamed of being loved, and then she discovered the greatest love of all in Yeshua of Nazaret, through whom she learned of the love of her heavenly Father.

As a little girl, she dreamed of being married and having children. Husband Tom and their children—David, Emily, and Ashley—are the precious fulfillment of that dream. And there have been the added gifts of in-laws—Tom, Greg, and Martha—and grandchildren: Lexy, Megan, Isabella, Lucas, Ava Grace, and Mica Rose.

Priscilla dreamed of being a missionary to Africa. Numerous visits to the continent and frequent African guests at her home provided opportunities to tell of the wonders of the heavenly Father.

She dreamed of having a farm where hope and healing would abound. The state of Virginia provides the setting for this great gift.

All these dreams have come true! To God be the glory; great things he has done!